TRADEHOUSE HOUSTON LLC

ADVANCED TECHNICAL ANALYSIS

A GUIDE TO HIGH PROBABILITY TRADING BY ALIGNING WITH SMART MONEY

JON FIBONACCI

Advanced Technical Analysis:

A Guide to High Probability Trading by Aligning with Smart Money

A Tradehouse Houston LLC book

eBook ISBN 978-1-7364341-1-6

Paperback ISBN 978-1-7364341-0-9

Published in the United States

For Amanda, Dale, and their son Charles LeFevre for always showing me that there is much more to life than money.

Also, special thanks to many of my trading mentors, Ashraf Laidi, Chris Lori, George Angell, Jack D. Schwager, Jake Bernstein, Jesse Livermore, John J. Murphy, Larry Williams, Linda Raschke, Laurence A. Connors, Lee Lowell, Mark Douglas, Nomi Prins, Paul Tudor Jones, Paula T. Webb, Richard Dennis, Richard D. Wyckoff, Sam Seiden, W. D. Gann, and many others. Without their knowledge and experience, I would not be the trader that I am.

Finally, a remarkable thanks to my best friends Aaron Toval and Catherine Evans, MSRS, CMD for their 15+ years of friendship and continued support since we were kids.

"Work hard to become smart so that one day you may be smart enough not to work hard."

-Jon Fibonacci

RISK DISCLOSURE

TRADING IS NOT SUITABLE FOR EVERYONE. Be sure to research prior to participating. Trading may result in complete loss of funds.

FOREIGN CURRENCY TRADING IS HIGHLY SPECULATIVE AND RISKY.

IT IS ONLY SUITABLE FOR THOSE WHO UNDERSTAND, AND ARE WILLING TO TAKE ON, THE FINANCIAL AND OTHER RISKS INVOLVED, AND WHO HAVE THE RESOURCES TO WITHSTAND LOSSES THAT MAY BE SIGNIFICANTLY GREATER THAT ANY DEPOSITS YOU HAVE MADE.

Financial instruments that are traded on leverage carry a high level of risk and you could lose more than your deposits.

Trading on a leveraged basis means a small market movement will have a proportionally larger impact on your position and could result in a total loss of your deposit(s).

The high leverage associated with trading foreign currency can result in significant losses due to price changes, especially during periods of volatility in the underlying market.

Please ensure you fully understand the risks and carefully consider your financial situation and trading experience before trading.

Trading forex on margin carries a high level of risk and may not be suitable for all investors. Before participating in the forex market, carefully consider your investment objectives, level of experience, and risk appetite.

You should trade in foreign currency contracts only if you understand the contracts (and contractual relationships) into which you are entering and the extent of your exposure to risk.

The possibility exists that you could sustain a loss of some or all of your initial investment and therefore **you should not invest money that you cannot afford to lose.**

The high degree of leverage associated with trading currencies means that the degree of risk compared to other financial products is higher.

The leveraged nature of forex trading means that any market movement will have an equally proportional effect on your deposited funds.

Leverage, or margin trading, may work against you resulting in substantial loss.

There is considerable exposure to risk in any off-exchange foreign exchange transaction, including, but not limited to, leverage, creditworthiness, limited regulatory protection, and market volatility that may substantially affect the price, or liquidity of a currency or currency pair.

You should be aware of all the risks associated with foreign exchange trading.

There is no recommendation to trade with live funds using the concepts from this book. Do not read this book and then trade with live funds.

Seek advice from an independent financial advisor if you have any doubts.

Advanced Technical Analysis:
A Guide to High Probability Trading by Aligning with Smart Money

Prefix

Prefix

After studying the markets for seven years, going through many mentors, books, and videos, I have put this book together. My trading career since the beginning of 2014 has been indescribable. The journey has been no less than life changing. My inspiration was derived from multiple individuals, some well-known to the trading community and others that have lived and passed. The concepts described in these chapters have been tested on the battlefield and have proven to bring favorable results. I am not a licensed financial advisor, just a guy who exploits the movements of theoretical smart money.

This book will take a lot of time and energy to grasp. What I am about to explain is not easy to understand the first time around. You will have to work and study. Many people will not read this all the way through, and those of you who do make it to the end will probably do it again. The information available to the public is not always reliable. Retail traders are cycled in and out of the markets on an endless loop (trust me, I see it happen every year). The goal of mine is to provide insight that most people do not know about. I have put together the best information I have ever come across, as well as my own experiences, and hope it serves readers well. There are no trend lines, shapes, indicators, or classic candlestick patterns. This is not an end-all-be-all type of book. However, it should be greatly beneficial to you on your journey as a trader and investor. For the sake of the reader, I hope you are open-minded and coachable.

Let the learning begin. Good luck.

Chapter 1

What Traders Need to Know

Learning Objectives

➢ Why most traders lose money

➢ How can a trader avoid the common pitfalls

I am sure everyone is well aware by now, but just in case you are not, I will tell you anyway. A quick search on the internet will tell you that the majority of traders lose money. This is based on historical data, not people's opinions. There are many mistakes made by the masses. We will cover those mistakes and how to avoid them in this chapter. It will set a strong foundation for the rest of the book. Our house will be built upon a rock so that when the storms of trading come, and they will come, our house will stand tall and not be washed away like the houses built on sand.

Everyone wants to know when the market will move and where it will go next. Of course, if we knew the answers consistently, we could quit our jobs and become self-sufficient traders and pull from the market every month like the very few who do. It can be done; however, I will disclose that it is difficult. If you are looking for a solution that is quick and easy, you might as well put down the book now and go on about your business. Very few people made real wealth taking the easy route. The strategies and context in this book will take some open-mindedness on your part and some personal studying. So let us get to it!

Why most traders lose money

Lack of a trading plan

Benjamin Franklin once stated, "If you fail to plan, you are planning to fail." As with any business, there are plans and procedures in place to allow the highest chance of success. When we go to work, our employer has many rules. They plan on you showing up on time, dressed appropriately, be productive, and follow the company guidelines. Trading is just like a business. There should be thorough instructions to follow so you can allow yourself not only to survive in the markets, but to thrive. Traders tend to lose quickly because they go into the markets with no plan. A lack of planning ultimately leads to failure.

Trading without risk management

In my opinion, the number one rule in trading is risk management. Beginner traders usually will overleverage their accounts in a trade and end up losing a large portion of their accounts in a short amount of time. Trading in this type of manner is pure gambling. In the early 1600's Miguel de Cervantes wrote: "It is the part of a wise man to keep himself today for tomorrow, and not venture all his eggs in one basket." This serves professional traders well as they can sustain losses but continue trading, unlike the novice who loses too much too quickly.

Relying on someone else for their success

On an airplane, we put our faith in the pilots to land us safely. We do not get to control the aircraft as we are not professionals. Chat rooms, messenger applications, and underground applications are not a good source of professional information. As discussed, the majority of traders lose. It is not wise to trust trade ideas from those who have not established themselves as successful traders. You are responsible for your capital and nobody else is to blame for your losses or to take credit for your gains. "In the long run, we shape our lives, and we shape ourselves. The process never ends until we die. And the choices we make are ultimately our own responsibility." claimed Eleanor Roosevelt.

Not understanding how markets move or what the markets are made of

Stocks, Bonds, Currency, and Commodities are different; however, they do share similarities. The novice trader is not aware of such differences in volatility, margin requirements, or even the profit or loss per point. The same-sized position on Gold as a currency pair could yield drastically different outcomes. When traders take big losses, they are often wondering what happened and quickly look for a reason why they lost. Some markets move at different times of the day and at different times of the year. Many traders have no idea these qualities even exist. Kofi Annan quipped "Knowledge is power. Information is liberating. Education is the premise of progress, in every society, in every family."

Quitting too easily and too early

It makes complete sense that traders would stop trading if they sustained heavy losses repeatedly. I do not blame them for taking the most logical route possible, but I do think trading is worth looking at again. If we were to quit dating after one relationship, that would be absurd! Just because your first trading experience may have been negative, it does not mean it will continue to be that way. If you need to take a break, then take some time away. Quitting, however, is unacceptable. One day in the future you may look back upon something you quit and wish you had stayed. I do not want you to regret such decisions. If others have done it, I am willing to bet you are capable, too. In Wealth for All: Living a Life of Success at the Edge of Your Ability, Idowu Koyenikan wrote: "If you quit on the process, you are quitting on the result."

Having Unrealistic Expectations

It is obvious many people want to get into the markets to acquire wealth. One of the problems is that some may believe in getting rich overnight, a highly unrealistic possibility. It can happen but is unlikely to occur. Any skill worth obtaining takes time and practice, and you must be willing to allow yourself time to get where you want to be. The media, which I often suggest to my friends and family not to watch, are full of stories that are abnormal to regular people. Success stories are wonderful, but many times happen to a small percentage of people. Remember, if something sounds too good to be true, it probably is.

Live trading without practice on paper money first

Trading can be exciting for new people. You can make or lose money in a matter of moments. Live trading is different from paper money as you are trading real money, but without first practicing what it is like to place trades, it will be hard seeing consistency. For those who played sports, we practiced all week before we played in a real game. Going into an official game without practicing first is a recipe for disaster. In Master of Stupidity, Toba Beta claimed "Practice doesn't make perfect. Practice reduces the imperfection."

Trading based on emotions

I think we can all agree that humans have emotions. We feel sadness, happiness, loneliness, fear, love, greed, and many others. These emotions can often get in the way of success in trading. Fear can make a trader leave a winning, or losing, position early. Greed can force a trader into holding a winner too long, and result in the winner becoming a loser. Many combinations will negatively affect the trader's account if the trading is run by emotional-based decisions. In life, emotions can often lead us into trouble, like when we argue with someone and say something we do not mean. The heat of the moment can have life-changing effects, in both life and trading.

How can a trader avoid the common pitfalls?

Build a trading plan and follow it

Who, what, where, when, and why? Those are the common questions we can apply to a trading plan. What assets are going to be traded? Think about which ones you want to trade and list them. When are you going to trade? The New York open or the London open? The choice is up to each person and it is a good idea to know when the markets are likely to move. This paragraph should have given you some clues!

Trade with strict risk management

Conservative risk management is considered 1-2% risk per trade. This means on any given trade, the most one is willing to lose is 1% or 2% of the overall account. So for example, on a $1,000 account, 2% risk would be risking $20 maximum on the trade. The loss should not exceed $20. With a loss, the account would still have $980 left to trade another day. Those who lost more would struggle to get it back since they would have to make more, potentially leading to overleveraging and losing the account on a bad trade. Yikes!

Do not rely on social media or television for answers

Best explained in the chapter on manipulation, I can let you in on a little secret. The media is not in your best interest. Public opinion is also generally wrong. Do not be a sheep led by other sheep but rather be your own Shepard. Learn a lot, study, read, and obtain knowledge for you to make your own sound decisions. If needed, find a successful mentor, and ask for guidance. Although I will admit it may cost money, some can be worth well beyond the initial costs. Independent thinkers tend to do better in life than others, in my opinion.

Understand how the markets move and what they are made of

The markets go from consolidation to expansion. Some assets, like commodities, can consolidate for a long period of time, whereas currency may be more volatile. We get more into how the markets move throughout the book, especially the chapter on manipulation. Major currency pairs tend to move fewer points than cross pairs, so be careful about your position size.

The U.S. Dollar Index is a basket of currencies, made up of Euros, Pounds, Yen, and more. One thing about the Index is that the basket is measured by different weights. For example, the GBP (Great British Pound) holds a different weight percentage than the Yen. At the time this book is written, the Euro holds the biggest weight at 57.6% (Coghlan). This information is crucial to understanding the correlation divergence.

Balance life and trading to not burn yourself out

We all have our own life to live. Too much of one thing can have a negative effect. For example, too much candy can bring a stomachache. The markets have been around longer than we have and will be around longer than us. It is ok to take breaks and reconvene another time. Your mind needs to be healthy and sharp to remain focused.

Have realistic expectations

You will take losses trading the markets. There is simply no way around it. Time, energy, focus, and capital is a requirement for success in the markets. Understand that true wealth is built over a large amount of time. Warren Buffet said it best when he stated, "Someone is sitting in the shade today because someone planted a tree a long time ago."

Trade paper money before trading live capital

I would gladly recommend gaining all the experience you can out of trading a paper money account. This was you can play around with the order types and other functions of your platform. When trading live capital, you may need to perform actions that may be considered complex to novice traders, such as taking partial profits, setting a stop loss in profit, and other things. This is also a good way to measure roughly how much you would win or lose if the trade were to be taken real. However, I will advise, that trading live is much different than demo as demo accounts usually have low spreads and do not have slippage as they are not real trades.

Eliminate trading based on emotions

As human beings, we have emotions. Telling you to not have them would be an impossible task. However, I urge you to not place trades or manage trades based on emotions. More specifically, fear and greed. Fear can prevent you from even getting into the trade in the first place. Greed can leave you hanging onto a trade too long and not taking profits. Trading should be done through technical and/or fundamental analysis and should have nothing to do with emotions. Letting a loss run in fear of taking a loss can lead to losing far beyond what you originally anticipated. If you are wrong, you are wrong. Take a small loss and move on. If you think the market will turn against you, take your profits and be content with that. There will be new opportunities in the future.

References

Beta, Toba. Master of Stupidity. 2011.

Koyenikan, Idowu. Wealth for All: Living a Life of Success at the Edge of Your Ability. Grandeur Touch, LLC, 2016.

Coghlan, Giles. "How the US Dollar Index Can Help Your Trading." ForexLive, www.forexlive.com/Education/!/how-the-us-dollar-index-can-help-your-trading-20190126.

Chapter 2

Market Manipulation

Learning Objectives

➤ Who controls price

➤ Why price is manipulated

➤ When is price likely to be manipulated

This chapter may be the most important, as it should shift your entire perspective about the financial markets and how the markets actually work. Do you carry around your life savings in cash? Probably not. Most people who have money either have it in the markets, or the markets by means of a retirement plan like a 401(k), or savings accounts and CDs. There are some people who have loads of cash sitting in their sock drawer, in a shoebox, or under the bed but that does not represent the majority of cases. The money is sitting in various banks or large institutions. The banks are the ones who control the mass amounts of money. Banks like J.P. Morgan & Chase, Citi Bank, Barclays, and more. *"The greatest volume of currency is traded in the interbank market. This is where banks of all sizes trade currency with each other and through electronic networks. Big banks account for a large percentage of total currency volume trades. Banks facilitate forex transactions for clients and conduct speculative trades from their own trading desks."* *(Segal)*

Now that we have established who has the most money in the game, we next need to establish what they would like to do with all that cash. Well, a bank is still a business, and businesses are trying to turn a profit, so it is safe to say they want to do the same. It takes serious money to move markets. They are the ones who have the power to bend price and move it however they see fit. Imagine wet clay spinning on a turntable and when the artist places their hand on the clay, it slowly shapes into a beautiful piece of artwork like a vase or flowerpot. Only in the world of finance, the clay is price movements, and the artists are the banks. Retail traders do not move the markets in large increments. Remember everyone's money is in the bank and small traders are controlling only a minuscule percentage of the cash, which would equivalate a drop of water in the ocean.

Maybe you do not believe me yet and that is ok. The charts are for convincing you at the end of the chapter but do not skip to the charts just yet. I believe it to be crucial that you understand the underlying context of the reasoning behind what you are going to witness. I know you want to get to a "light bulb" moment in your trading if you have not gotten some already but just be patient. It is hard but you can do it, I promise.

For those of you who have been trading for a while now are probably familiar with traditional technical analysis patterns like flags, breakouts, trend lines, and such. If I told you those were repeatedly exploited by larger players than you, would you think I was lying? If I said the bigger sharks wanted to swallow the smaller fish for tonight's dinner, would you consider trusting my statement? I believe that to be the continuous reality of the financial markets. The rich keep getting richer and the poor stay poor, but why? It is because of market manipulation. Essentially, what is happening is that you are being forced out of your trade on purpose. Woah is that legal?! Well… Not necessarily legal, but it happens regardless. Let us dig deeper. Let us take a gander at some previous real-world examples of someone getting caught red-handed at manipulating markets before we look at pattern exploitation.

"In late 2019, the department of justice charged another former JPMorgan Chase & Co executive with alleged racketeering and manipulating precious metals between 2008 and 2016" *(Reuters)*. Jeffery Ruffo's case relates to what is known as spoofing, an illegal practice of placing orders in the market with no intention of executing them to influence prices. I would suggest reading more into spoofing online if you would like to head further into the nitty-gritty of that topic, which is usually a crime associated with organized crime like the mafia or cartel. Yes, I just compared the financial banks to mobsters. They are the *real* gangsters in this day and age.

If you were to search online on how to trade forex, I am certain you would come across many websites that are willing to teach you for free or even for a small fee. The free content provided on these websites is utterly useless. Why would I tell you that? First of all, I know what those websites have because I have seen them for myself. Secondly, according to many trusted online sources and broker statements, the majority of traders actually lose money. If information is readily available online, why would most traders lose money?

The market price tends to move to areas where orders that have not been triggered are sitting. This is found either below or above the current market price, or both. The type of orders I am referring to are known as buy stops, sell stops, stop losses, and trailing stops. I like to use general areas to mark up these levels on my personal charts and if I notice a reaction from the area, I will look to enter the market.

Once the pending orders have been hit and liquidity is no longer available in the price area, it should reverse from current levels. This can oftentimes set the low or high of that particular trend and fine-tuning the entry into the market can set up a trader for some nice rewards on minimal risk. This can occur on all time frames, but will appear more on smaller time frames than large ones, obviously.

Let us review just a couple of retail price action patterns that are commonly used amongst the retail trading universe, which from now on we will call "dumb money" (opposite of the banks referred to as smart money). First, let us take a look at the double-bottom formation. It is basically when the market has made two low points relatively close together.

"Double-bottom formation"

- Commonly referred to as support in the dumb money universe
- Traders will place buy orders around this area or slightly above it with a stop loss below the lows
- The "Double-top formation" will work the same way, but everything is reversed

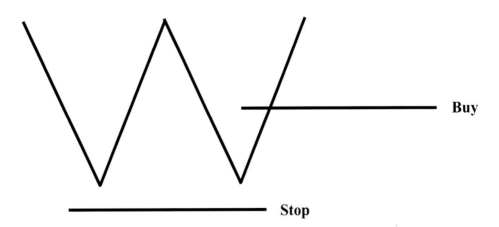

This is the main idea in the retail universe, and this is not how I place my trades. Where the stop loss is placed is where I try to enter the market for a buying opportunity, when other traders are getting stopped out. In a market environment where *96% of traders lose money,* I definitely do not want to be doing what they are doing, but rather the opposite (Russell). I want to observe the dumb money and take the contrarian approach to the markets. *"Contrary-opinion traders are always looking for a one-sided market sentiment in order to take the opposite side. If you remember that the crowd in invariably wrong at the extremes in the market, you will likely do better by taking a position opposite to the majority opinion than to follow the crowd."* (Angell, page 58)

Now, we will take a look at what really happens in the market under usual circumstances. I would also like to convey that George Angell also wrote *"The reason why some traders why away from placing stop-loss orders is that many floor traders have a tendency to "gun" for stops. That is, they estimate that many stop-loss orders exist just below the market, and they try to run the market down the "take out" or activate the stops, and then run the price back up again."* (Angell, page 130). The following illustration shows a visual of what he is referring to, which I believe is remarkably similar to the Wyckoff Schematic.

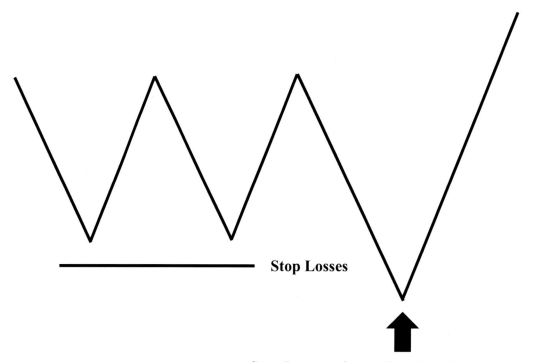

Stop Losses

Stop Losses triggered and traders are taken out of the market and price reverses

EUR/USD 1HR JANUARY 14, 2020

EUR/USD 15MIN DECEMBER 17, 2019

Hopefully, you are able to recognize that price can move in accordance with the examples explained throughout this chapter. Just as the market can run stops on the downside, do not forget they can be run on the upside above double-top formations. With your new perspective on the market, you are now encouraged to look back in your own charts to see for yourself what happens in the markets. Although I am only giving you two examples of this type of price manipulation, it should be enough to spark your interest and to take your learning further by studying charts outside of this literature. For anyone who has been frustrated as to why your analysis was correct, but you were stopped out before the market turned in your favor, you now have the answer as to why it happened. In my opinion, this tends to occur most often during the London session and during the London/US overlap session.

Chapter Conclusion and final thoughts

It is to my best understanding that:

- *Markets are manipulated for stops*

- *Retail traders do not control price*

- *The London session and US overlap provide opportunities to trade this environment*

 - *The "running of stops" provides low risk and high reward trading opportunities*

- *96% of traders lose money so we observe the masses and do the opposite*

- *You cannot believe everything you see on the internet (free charting schools)*

- *If trading were as easy as googling images, everyone would be rich*

References

Angell, George. Winning in the Commodities Market: A Moneymaking Guide to Commodity Futures Trading. Doubleday & Co, 1979.

Reuters. "U.S. Charges Another Ex-JPMorgan Executive with Alleged Market Manipulation." 16 Nov. 2019, www.reuters.com/article/us-usa-metals-charges/u-s-charges-another-ex-jpmorgan-executive-with-alleged-market-manipulation-idUSKBN1XP2FQ.

Russell, John. "Prevent Losses in Your Forex Trading." The Balance, The Balance, 25 June 2019, www.thebalance.com/why-do-forex-traders-lose-money-1344936.

Sanderson, Henry. "Three JPMorgan Metals Traders Charged with Market Manipulation." Subscribe to Read | Financial Times, Financial Times, 16 Sept. 2019, www.ft.com/content/2d7be5a6-d87a-11e9-8f9b-77216ebe1f17.

Segal, Troy. "Forex Folk: Who Trades Currency and Why." Investopedia, 29 Jan. 2020, www.investopedia.com/articles/forex/11/who-trades-forex-and-why.asp.

Chapter 3

Institutional Candles

Learning Objectives

➢ What is an institutional candle

➢ Why institutional candles are important

A common type of trading strategy in the community of investing is a term called "Supply and Demand." In short, it means to buy low and sell high. I know, you have probably heard that before. I have observed that both young and experienced traders do not buy when price is low, or short when price is high. In reference to hindsight market structure, it is easy to tell when price was high or low. I can tell that many traders cannot truly tell what the market is doing most of the time. Many cannot tell when price is high or low, or in the terms I like to use, at extremes.

As outlined in chapter one, retail speculators do not move the markets. Even If I took the money from my entire neighborhood and put it in one trade, the price of a stock or currency pair would not move. It takes an exorbitant amount of capital to move the price of a stock, commodity, or currency pair. I am talking about an enormous amount of capital. Only banks or financial institutions have this amount of money. *Institutional investors face fewer protective regulations because it is assumed, they are more knowledgeable and better able to protect themselves. There are generally six types of institutional investors: endowment funds,*

commercial banks, mutual funds, hedge funds, pension funds and insurance companies (Chen). I

am also certain that lines on a chart do not move price. Lines are subjective! Everyone draws

them at different points and different angles; therefore, trend lines are not reliable. I have seen so

many traders draw different lines around the same levels of price action. To wrap it up, the

answer is simple. Trend lines do not move markets either. It may work for someone once in a

while but often show no levels of consistency. After all, if the market did not show some level of

ability to generate profits, nobody would be willing to trade.

In my experience, another tactic that has not proven successful without proper context is

the use of harmonic patterns. Harmonic patterns are basic math, but it is the same math as

Fibonacci retracements and extensions. The Fibonacci retracement and extension tools are

something that I use in my trading, but I do not blindly throw them on my charts. The patterns

used are supposedly "bullish" or "bearish" but why would you rely on a tool to tell you that?

When it comes to technical analysis, there are many concepts that I look for when I want

to place a trade. I try to place my trades in an area where I believe the institutions are trading. In

short, I want to align myself with them and want to have the same trades they do. Learning when

and where they trade is crucial. I do not look for trend lines, nor do I look for harmonics or

cypher patterns. I look for accumulation or distribution clues left in price action. In other words,

a more advanced "supply and demand."

Where would the banks be placing buy and sell orders? Well, we have got some context to

go through before I can explain where the better trading would be done. Learning a new skill

takes time and honest dedication. Many traders who ask for help only want a simple answer or simple formula they can just take and apply to the markets, but trading is more complex than that.

Let us think back for a second. I mentioned previously that banks and institutions are the ones who control prices. From now on, we will just refer to them as "Smart Money." Smart money is the capital that is being controlled by institutional investors, market mavens, central banks, funds, and other financial professionals (Banton). They are the ones with the most amount of cash. They own amounts of money so large they can afford large amounts of drawdown. I will say this part again just to make sure we cover everything. Smart money can take drawdown. Not every player in the market is trying to buy the exact bottom or short at the exact top. Getting into massive positions takes some time. It could take days, weeks, or even months. As a small speculator, none of us should ever dream of holding a losing trade for weeks or months. Smart money can, and they do. They need time to fill all the orders they are placing into the markets. They do not buy everything they want in one day. This happens among all of the tradable asset classes.

Now, after smart money accumulates enough to push price in the opposite direction, a new high or new low should form. This is the market showing you a willingness to go higher or lower. However, this is not where I have been trading. Once a new high or low is made, I wait for a pullback to enter. The plan is to ride most of the move that is supposed to be coming next. I usually pick my profit targets at a bearish price if I am bullish or a bullish price if I am short. We will discuss risk management in a later portion of this text but for now, I will leave you with this. My minimum risk to reward ratio is always 1:3. However, it can be as high a 1:10 or more. Trading these candlesticks in the right environment allows me to do so.

Imagine swimming in the ocean. Is it not harder to swim against the current than with it? When you align your trades with smart money, you are basically swimming with the tide, not against it. It is a simple, famous concept and applies to a lot of scenarios in life, including trading. You do not want to be on the wrong side of the market, which is the side against smart money. I will not say you cannot have profitable trades going against the market, but over time it is not going to work well in the majority of cases. Let the smart money players move price in your favor for you. When I place a trade, I do not remain stagnant, watching the computer. I go about my regular life. I am relying on the big players to push price so I may profit too.

In a bullish market, when price begins to trade lower after a new high has been established, I want to look at how price left the previous low. Did it move in a casual manner? A casual manner would indicate normal candlesticks. Did it move with force? Big up candles? Determining how significant the pricing level at the bottom of the up leg is particularly important. This will tell you the degree in the market popularity of the previous price. If the level was left in a violent manner, or explosive price, this means there is an exceedingly high demand for that pricing level. When the market pulls back into a previous level of strong demand, it is likely the market is wanting to accumulate a few more orders before repricing higher. This is where I like to be entering a long position. I usually get a little drawdown, if any. Although I admit that I do take losses.

The next question I want to answer for you is "where am I supposed to get in?" What is supposed to be my set entry price for a long position? You must look at the down candlesticks prior to the explosive move. Why the down candle or series of candles? We just discussed that smart money is buying as price is moving down. They are the ones buying price as it goes lower. In essence, the orders they are placing are the ones inside the down candle or candles. Normally,

I like to see one nice sized candle with small wicks. I want to enter somewhere between the open and the close of the down candle. This could range in the number of points based on which time frame you are trading. A down candle on a monthly time frame could be 100 points, but a daily down candle might only be 40. Obviously, different assets are more volatile than others; therefore, it is going to vary on numerous factors. When the range is larger, I prefer to "cut the candle in half" and find the midway point between the open and close. Normally, I would do this on a weekly and monthly candlestick, although I have done it on the daily. If the criteria are met, the ideal scenario would be for price to enter the range of the down close candle and then spike higher from there. If the price of the asset goes down to the body close, the trade might not go as planned. The market did not react the way I expected, and I would have been wrong. I would cut the loss short and move on. For an ideal risk to reward, I would do the simple math and make the range of the down candlestick 1% of my account If I were to enter at the top of the body as price is coming down. If I am wrong, I lose just 1% of the account and walk away. Profit targets for these types of trades can be upwards of 5% or more so they are worth trading. If I listed the top 10 best trades of my career, 8 of them would be from this concept of a more advanced version of "supply and demand."

We have been reviewing a bullish scenario and it would be the exact opposite if trading the bearish scenario. I would look for an up candle prior to a strong selloff instead of a down candle before a strong rally. It will take time to trust the concept enough to put live money on the trade. Trust comes from understanding the concept and seeing it happen repeatedly. If you need to make a demo account and practice trading this type of supply and demand, I highly encourage you to do that. Not every move in the market is going to work. Factors such as where price is in a given range or trend make a difference as well. If you are trying to buy after price has rallied for a good amount of time, it is likely your trade will not pan out in your favor. The overall market probably needs to have a deeper level of pullback, or retracement. I keep all levels of time frame in mind, to solidify the level of probability I am evaluating. The goal is to trade high probability setups and you will not fully grasp it until you have had some experience.

Now let us go over some risk management strategies. Many traders quit after a short period of time because they cannot figure out how to generate profits. Young traders make all the mistakes and do not fully understand what they are doing. My trading requires low risk and high reward. In situations where I am right on one trade, but wrong in the next, I can still be profitable. I see far too often traders holding losing positions thinking the market will "come back eventually." Sometimes it will, sometimes it will not. If it does not, you are leaving your entire account at risk, which is why traders blow their accounts. Losing all your money in one single trade is devastating. I get price action wrong sometimes but that does not mean I am out of the trading game. I could be wrong three or four times in a row and still have 96% of my account ready to go. Trading with the supply and demand concepts that I have provided to you will allow you to minimize your risk and maximize your reward. In the end, we are all in this to make money, right? Next, my favorite part of trading books - the charts.

USD/CAD *"Loonie"* Daily in February of 2019

Notice:

- 4 days of noticeable up movement

- Market returns slowly back to the origin of the move (the last down candle)

- Price reacts and the next couple of weeks are *explosive!*

NZD/USD *"Kiwi"* Weekly in December of 2019

Notice:

- Solid up closing candle prior to strong selloff (6 weeks of down closing candles)

- Price reaches into the last up candle and reacts

- Price trades significantly lower after a return to the origin of the previous move lower

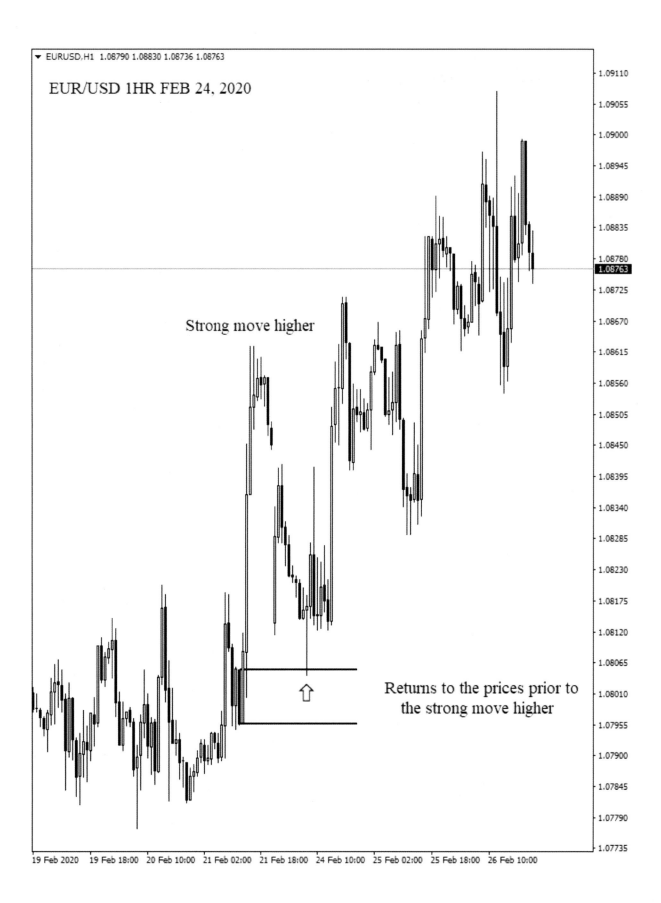

EUR/USD 1HR FEB 24, 2020

Strong move higher

Returns to the prices prior to
the strong move higher

EUR/USD "Fiber" 1HR NOVEMBER 22, 2019

Returns to previous prices prior to strong move lower

Strong move lower

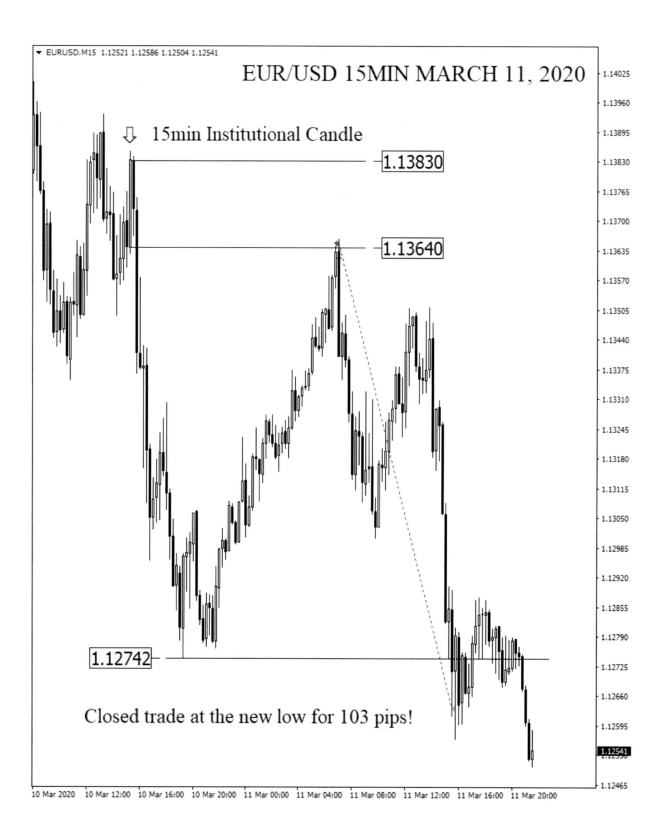

EUR/USD 15MIN MARCH 11, 2020

⬇ 15min Institutional Candle

1.13830

1.13640

1.12742

Closed trade at the new low for 103 pips!

Final Thoughts

Now that you have seen the power of institutional candles, it would be wise to review your own charts and see if you can point them out. Do not believe in every single move in the market. Remember, it is about the strength of the move afterward that helps determine whether smart money is behind the movement or not. These candles can produce small risk and large rewards in the marketplace. The Euro trade on March 11, 2020, brought me almost a 5% gain on the overall account in one trade. Not bad for one day of work and I spent most of the time asleep!

References

Banton, Caroline. "Smart Money Is Invested by Those in the Know." Investopedia, Investopedia, 29 Jan. 2020, www.investopedia.com/terms/s/smart-money.asp.

Chen, James. "Institutional Investor." Investopedia, Investopedia, 29 Jan. 2020, www.investopedia.com/terms/i/institutionalinvestor.asp.

Chapter 4

Correlation Divergence

Learning objectives

➤ What is a correlation divergence

➤ Why is the correlation divergence important

➤ Price action examples

Before we begin

The insight I am about to share with you would not have been possible without the help of some of my mentors. The two that have helped me the most with this content are Larry Williams and George Angell. The same Larry Williams who wrote *The Secret of Selecting Stocks for Immediate and Substantial Gains (1986)* and won the World Cup Trading Championships® in 1987 with over 11,000% gains during that year. Also, George Angell wrote numerous books on technical analysis, including *Winning in The Commodities Markets (1979)*. I would not have the knowledge I am divulging to you without first gaining the wisdom from these legendary traders and authors. Please support their work if you find yourself interested in this chapter. I am forever grateful.

What is a correlation divergence?

The answer is simple, it is in the name! It is a divergence of correlated assets. For example, when two assets that correlate with one another, or in another term "move together," fall out of correlation. One may tend to slightly move in a different direction than its peer. This can be seen often in indices such as the Standard and Poor's 500 Index, the Dow Jones Industrial Average, and the NASDAQ. It is difficult to see if you are not looking for this type of movement, so a trader needs to actively search for these particular criteria to hopefully get logical use from the formation. Another name for this type of analysis is called *relative strength analysis*.

Not only do the American Indices correlate, but there are also many other assets that move together. For Example, **EUR/USD** and **GBP/USD**, also known as *Fiber* and *Cable*. Although the correlation for these majors may not be as strong as others, it is still worth noting. The **AUD/USD** pair and **NZD/USD** pair, also known as *Aussie* and *Kiwi*, tend to correlate with one another strongly in most cases. In addition, Gold and Silver are often paralleled. Certain stocks may be compared to their respective sectors. For instance, ($AMZN) and NASDAQ (as of August 2020). The idea is to compare them to see which one is outperforming or underperforming the other. The analysis will provide insight as to which asset is strong or weak. It will assist in determining where potentially high probability trades may occur. A trader would ideally look for buying opportunities on assets that outperform their respective peers. This makes sense because you are buying something that would be considered strong and avoiding the weaker assets, otherwise known as *laggards*. The outperformer would be referenced as a *leader*. In a shorting scenario, the laggard would be ideal to short due to weakness.

Let us take a look at what exactly I am referring to. If we were to look at either a line chart or a candlestick chart, it would be a good idea to overlap the two assets which you have decided to pair up against one another. We would need to determine the outperformer and buy, or the underperformer and short, given whichever market conditions we are in. The image below is a visual representation of what we will be looking at in later charts.

Correlation Divergence Image 1

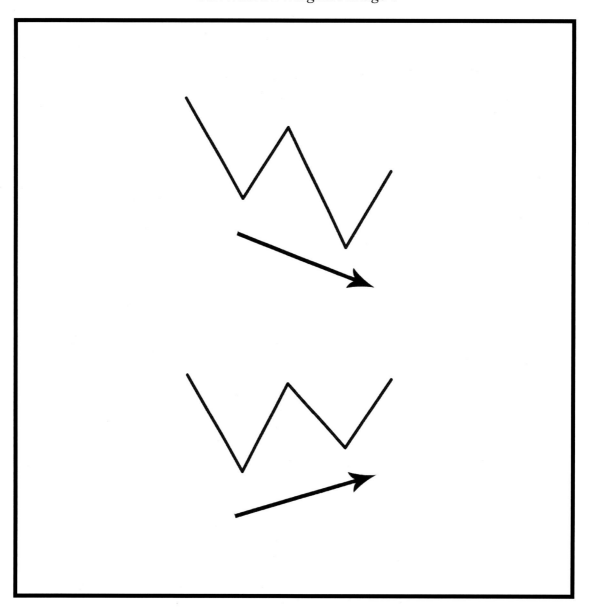

In this image, we can see the top asset is making a lower low while the bottom asset is making a higher low. Whichever the bottom asset is, that one is your leader. That is the asset you should be looking for potentially higher pricing. It is especially beneficial if it occurs on a small-time frame while the price is also at a higher time frame level of possible support. It could indicate a turn in the market. Retracements from here could be favorable to the trader looking for higher prices on that asset. Next, an example of EUR/USD and GBP/USD.

Correlation Divergence Image 2 provided by Tradingview.com

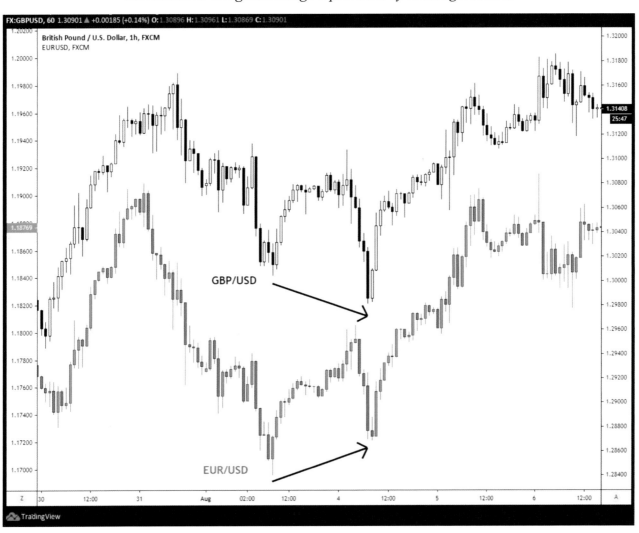

Notice how the EUR/USD made a higher low while GBP/USD was making a lower low? This is your correlation divergence! No indicators necessary, just simple chartwork. With my level of understanding, this means that more money (and by more money, I mean smart money) is favoring higher prices on EUR/USD. Notice anything else? Maybe an institutional candle in there somewhere? Pretty cool, isn't it? It is all starting to come together…

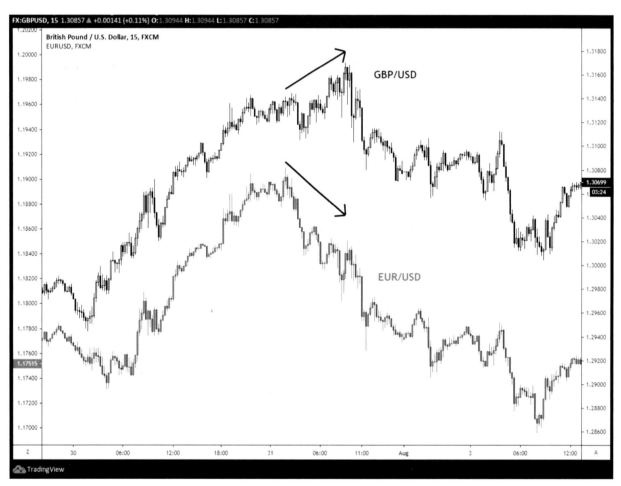

Correlation Divergence Image 3 provided by Tradingview.com

Let us look at the shorting example, above. Notice that EUR/USD in this case is underperforming relative to GBP/USD, giving a sign of weakness. The market then continues to sell off giving lower prices and profit potential to traders who shorted the market.

Why is the correlation divergence important?

By now you have witnessed some key turning points in the market. The importance of these divergences is that they will potentially create tops or bottoms in the marketplace. You may not be able to catch the absolute high or low but knowing when a potential trend change may take place could be beneficial to traders. I have witnessed these occur on most time frames.

The divergence I use in my own trading could be a new tool you may find useful in your own studying of the markets. I wish you may find it useful as it is one of my favorite tools. For now, I am sure many of you would like to see more examples, so I have included more. Enjoy!

Correlation Divergence Image 4 provided by Tradingview.com

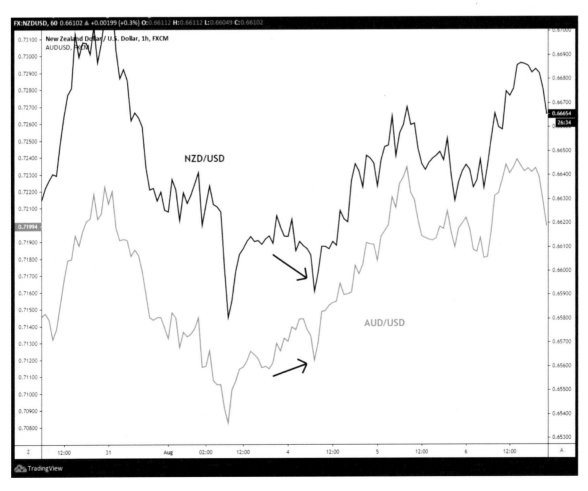

Correlation divergence Image 5 provided by Tradingview.com

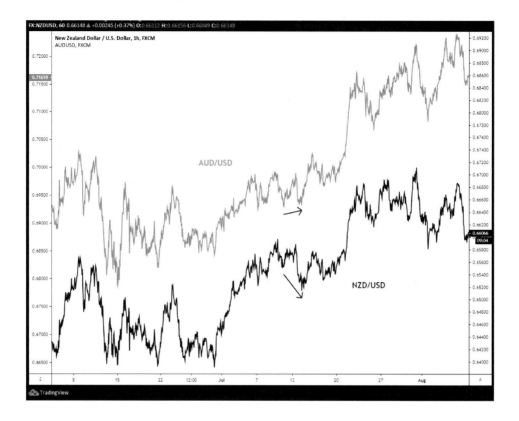

Correlation divergence Image 6 provided by Tradingview.com

The stock crash of 2020. People say you cannot time the market…

Do you agree?

Correlation divergence Image 7 provided by Tradingview.com

Correlation divergence Image 8 provided by Tradingview.com

While the Dow Jone was sliding lower, MSFT instead was able to create a higher low indicating that professional buying was taking place. The stock then rallied 70% from the low up the previous high.

From $135.90 - $231.65 (Sept. 2,2020)

Correlation divergence Image 9 provided by Tradingview.com

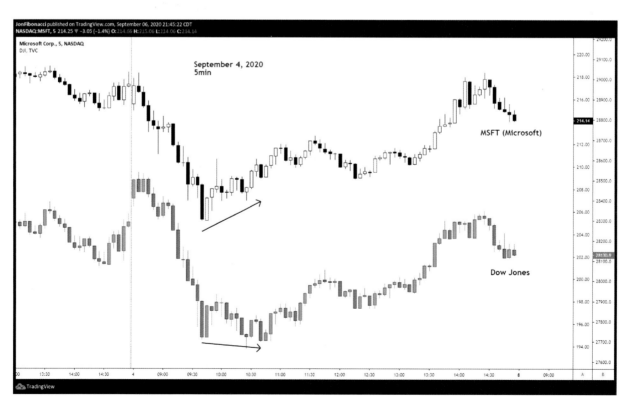

Correlation divergence Image 10 provided by Tradingview.com

Correlation divergence Image 11 provided by Tradingview.com

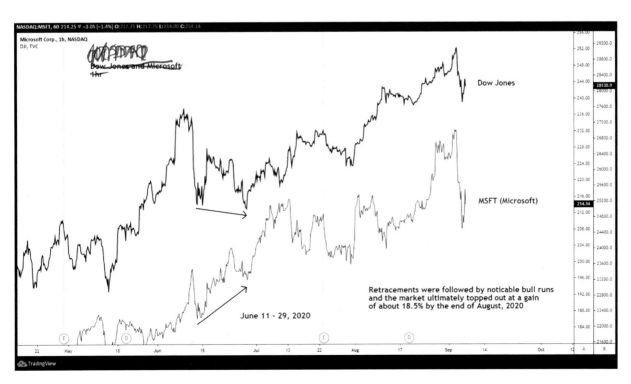

Correlation divergence Image 12 provided by Tradingview.com

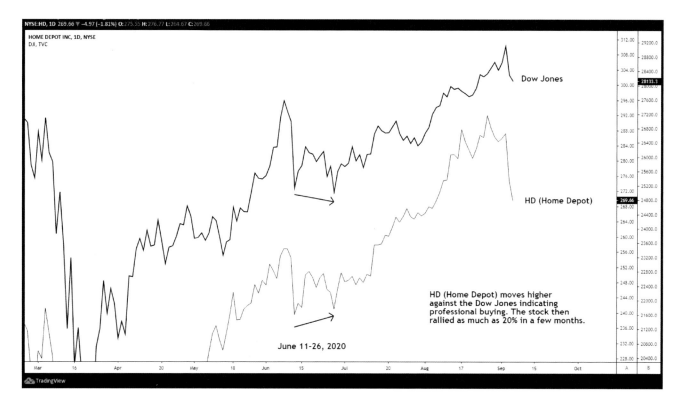

Correlation divergence Image 13 provided by Tradingview.com

Have you noticed the difference between the beginning charts and the later ones? Could you tell I started to add other concepts from this book into them... Cool, huh? I am sure that you noticed I placed a lot of examples on buying opportunities instead of selling opportunities. I did that because stocks are almost always overall bullish. However, there are selling or shorting opportunities that work the same exact manner, just opposite. I did leave two selling charts for reference, but it will now be up to you to go into your own charts and teach yourself. You did not think I would hand you *everything,* did you?

References

Angell, George. *Winning in the Commodities Market: A Money-Making Guide to Commodity Futures Trading*. Doubleday, 1979.

Williams, Larry R. *The Secret of Selecting Stocks for Immediate and Substantial Gains*. Windsor Books, 1986.

The next chapter has to do with psychology. Please note that I am not a psychologist. If you need psychological help, please reach out to a professional.

Chapter 5

Intro to Psychology

Learning Objectives

➢ Why psychology is important

➢ Success starts with your attitude

➢ Ideas to increase your chances of success

Defining your edge in the marketplace is important. It is the foundation on which a trading plan begins. However, no matter how great a trade plan or strategy may be, it will not be of any use to anyone without proper implementation. A fast car will not win a race without a skilled driver leading the way. Many traders experience what I refer to as psychological warfare. They are at war and most of them probably are not even aware of it. The battles, however, are not usually with the market, but rather themselves. There are many reasons traders enter the market and there are plenty of opportunities for success, but it is well known most do not find it. Only a small percentage of traders are consistently profitable. When beginner or intermediate traders start to lose, they easily blame someone or something else for their poor performance.

Almost all of my psychological success came from studying Mark Douglas and Paula T. Webb. If you have not read _Trading in the Zone_ by Mark Douglas, then I would highly recommend investing the time to do so. In addition to that, it would be a good idea to acquire his other book _The Disciplined Trader_. I know what you might be thinking. I give a lot of book recommendations. I simply cannot help it! Some of these people I believe are the best at what they do in their profession. Each one of them has helped me in their own way. I encourage all traders, novice or experienced, to study their materials for additional knowledge on the subject.

As someone thinks to themselves and decides their next venture in life, trading or not, they must choose whether they can or cannot. As Confucius once stated, *"The man who thinks he can and the man who thinks he can't are both right."* There are profitable traders in the world. It starts with an "I can" attitude. If your attitude is negative, then your results will most likely be negative. The first time someone told me that, I immediately disagreed without hesitation. I did not think my attitude would affect my trading if the strategy was good enough to turn a profit. However, over time I learned that it is not always about your strategy. Your attitude can affect your emotions, which can affect your decision-making process, which can affect your trades, which can ultimately affect your overall trading results. Napoleon Hill wrote that "Greatness comes to those who develop a burning desire to achieve high goals" in *Success Through a Positive Mental Attitude*. So success starts with your attitude.

You will face obstacles in trading. You will take losing trades. You may think the market will go higher and it ends up plummeting lower. You may think the market will top out and create a high, but it will continue to climb against your analysis. Given enough trades, at some point, you will get out of a position far earlier than you should have. You may think to yourself "I should have held on longer" or "I wish I were still in this trade." You will think about how much money you could have made and will not focus on how much you did make. How will you overcome these scenarios? What will your attitude be like? Will you ride an emotional rollercoaster through your trading career? Probably.

I have been there and to this day, after nearly seven years in the markets, I still have emotions. However, I know what to do given the market data and not make decisions based on what I am feeling. Do I and will I get it wrong? Yes, I am not perfect. I do follow specific guidelines outlined in my trading plan. If the market does this, I will do that. If the market does that, I will do this. There is a plan for all scenarios. If a new situation unfolds and I do not know what to do, I will collapse my trade and study.

The most important thing in my trading plan is capital preservation and risk management. Capital preservation meaning that I want to be around forever and not lose my entire account, or what most would call "blowing up an account." In my early years, I did blow up some forex accounts. I started with minuscule amounts of money since I was still a beginner. $200-300 USD each, which was small enough not to bankrupt me, but big enough to keep a young mind in attention to the marketplace. After working as a waiter and saving up $4,000 USD, I knew the value of a hard day's work and knew risking my whole savings in one go was a stupid idea. Right after turning tables for chump change, I joined the US Navy and that is what gave me the time to devote to studying the markets. How is that possible? Some might be wondering. It is easy! You *create* time. We all have the same 24 hours in a day.

Circling back to trading psychology and how we can stay around longer than the average trader. I think you would be surprised at the statistics behind what actually happens to traders. This is what happens to most of them! Do not be one of those people and end up a statistic. You are better than that! I promise to the very person reading this book, you are better than being a washout and a quitter. Growing up, many people treated me like I was or would be a washout and a quitter. From teachers who kicked me out of class repeatedly, to a cheating girlfriend, to bosses who fired me, to racist and sexist leadership in the Navy, to online hecklers, to hateful neighbors, you name it and I have probably experienced it in my 26 years on this planet. However, here I am, in my underwear, writing my first book. I am asked to teach thousands of traders and stream almost daily. Please trust me. You are better than how people say or treat you.

Ok, so back to trading psychology and how we can stay around longer than everyone else. The following information is provided so trader can avoid becoming a failed statistic. Well, you have to see what the losers are doing and avoid what they do at all costs. What are those traits? For starters, *over-leveraging*. This means that a trader will put on a huge position with no regard for managing risk. If the trade goes their favor, they stand to make a handsome return. However, if the trade goes against them, their account is toast. Typically, you can find these people flaunting on the internet that they doubled or tripled their account (or more) in a short amount of time. Have you ever noticed that these people cannot perform that way every week or every month? It is because they cannot. Otherwise, you would see them post about it! They will hide the fact that they took on a huge position and blew their account to save themselves the embarrassment.

How can you avoid becoming like them? Simple. Manage your risk. Personally, I keep my risk at a conservative 1-2% of my account per trade. More times than not at 1%. I am able to comfortably sleep at night knowing that the worst that can happen is losing 1% or maybe 1.5% if given enough slippage. I have never been slipped out of a position bad enough to lose more than that. It is possible, but it has never happened to me. In order to keep my risk between 1-2%, I do not hold trades over the weekend if I entered a position on a Friday. Sunday gaps can go well past your stop loss. If you find yourself waking up in the middle of the night to check your trade, you may be over-leveraging. If you watch your phone or check your trade every 5 minutes, you may need to check your risk management or ask yourself if you have truly accepted the risk you have taken. Here are some other ideas to increase your chances of success:

1) **Have a trading plan.** Detailed and written down. Use this as a guide to your trading and follow every rule without any deviation. Do NOT break your trading rules.

2) **Understand the risks** in trading and learn to be comfortable with the risk. This is why I risk small because that is what I am comfortable risking.

3) **Stay away from trading if you are experiencing a "bad day."** You know exactly what I am talking about. If you are not in the right frame of mind, do not trade. Come back when you are ready and can focus. This should save you from unnecessary losses.

4) **Get good sleep, eat right, and drink lots of water.** Do I need to explain this one? You know what being healthy does to your *body* and *mind*. Do you want the greatest chance of success? You have to set yourself up to win. Put down eating fast food every day. I know it sounds strange at first, but trust me, the healthy people in my life told me that and it worked well for me so it should work well for you too.

5) **Read Mark Douglas's books.** I put them in my book for a reason. One of my favorite things I learned from him is understanding that each trade in the market is unique. This means that just because I lost the last 2 or 3 trades does not mean the next trade will be a loser. They are all independent trades. This helps a lot when it comes to losing streaks, which I do believe will happen to us all at some point.

6) **Do not look at the money, look at the market.** Stop focusing on what you could make or lose and start focusing on what the market is telling you. You can even swap

your setting on MT4 around to display points instead of dollar amounts (yes, pun intended). This could be beneficial if you need it!

7) **Understand there will be more trading opportunities in the future.** Ok, so you missed a trade. Big deal! The market will provide another opportunity in the future. Just be patient and wait for the next setup. Do not dwell on the past. Leave the past in the past. You may miss another trade if you are too focused on the one you already missed!

8) **Do your own analysis.** Stop listening to everyone else and come to your own conclusion about the markets.

9) **Know your personality and trade based on your personality.** Would you expect a day trader and a position trader to take the same trades? No. Know who you are and trade what you are comfortable with. If you do not yet know what your trading personality is like, then you will figure it out in time. If you are an impatient person, maybe day trading is for you! If you only look at charts once or twice a week, position trading might be calling your name.

10) **Just because other people are trading does not mean you should be.** Cool, everyone else is posting trades or talking about trading but you cannot seem to find a trade worth taking. That is totally fine. Let others do what they have to do, and you will do what you have to do. Do not concern yourself with other people's results. Focus on your own career and avoid the noise.

11) **Turn off the television.** Stop listening to everyone else as mentioned earlier. You need to make independent choices about the markets. If the television gave sound advice, wouldn't we all be rich? Something to consider.

12) **Surround yourself with positivity.** We all need good friends. And by good, I am not referring to your drinking or smoking buddies. Good people as in ones who will help you when you need help. People who you can count on for sound advice about life or anything else. We uplift one another and inspire each other to do good, not waste our life away.

13) **Track your progress.** Using a trade journal and trading binder, it is a good idea to track where you are, so you know where you have been. You can study yourself and hopefully know where you need improvement. We all look at price history so why not look at your own history? Exactly.

14) **Always be a student.** When you stop learning, you are toast. Always be open to new ideas and learn as much as you can.

Final thoughts

You have reached the end of my psychology chapter. I hope you have enjoyed the content that I have provided and that my past experiences, along with my ideas, have helped you in a meaningful way. Remember to learn from your mistakes, as well as other people's mistakes. Do the best you can, and I am sure you will be fine.

References

Douglas, M. (1990). *The disciplined trader: Developing winning attitudes*. New York, NY: New York Institute of finance.

Douglas, M. (2000). *Trading in the Zone: Master the Market with Confidence, Discipline, and a Winning Attitude*. New York, NY: New York Institute of Finance.

Hill, N., 1999. *Success Through A Positive Mental Attitude*. Sydney: HarperBusiness.

Chapter 6

Open Interest

Learning Objectives

➢ What is Open Interest

➢ Where you can acquire Open Interest

"Open interest is the total number of outstanding derivative contracts, such as options or futures that have not been settled for an asset. The total open interest does not count and total every buy and sell contract. Instead, open interest provides a more accurate picture of the options trading activity, and whether money flows into the futures and options market are increasing or decreasing." (Ganti). Open interest can be found in the COT report, also known as the commitment of traders. This report is produced almost weekly from the Commodity Futures Trading Commission and can be found at https://www.cftc.gov/.

My level of understanding, based on Larry Williams's book (and what he was taught), is that a *decrease in open interest means commercials are releasing shorts* (bullish) and a *rise in open interest is an increase in shorts* (bearish). That book is *How I Made $1M Last Year Trading Commodities (1979)*. Normally, I do not pay attention to the open interest in terms of % increase or decrease as Larry teaches, but still have found good trading opportunities doing so. I look for obvious large moves up or down in open interest.

These "large moves" up or down are usually the moves that I like to rely on for setting tops or bottoms in the market. However, sometimes the market may consolidate and OI may move casually, but in one direction, indicating where price is likely to next. While I use OI, I do not use it alone. It is good to find correlation divergences as we reviewed in an earlier chapter. This is what adds to the probability of finding a directional bias on the higher time frame. I do not currently include other COT data in my analysis.

Let us review some charts where open interest played a big role. Some charts were used in my own trading and some were not. All charts for this chapter are courtesy of **Barchart.com** and I use their service for the purpose of open interest. All charts are on the daily time frame.

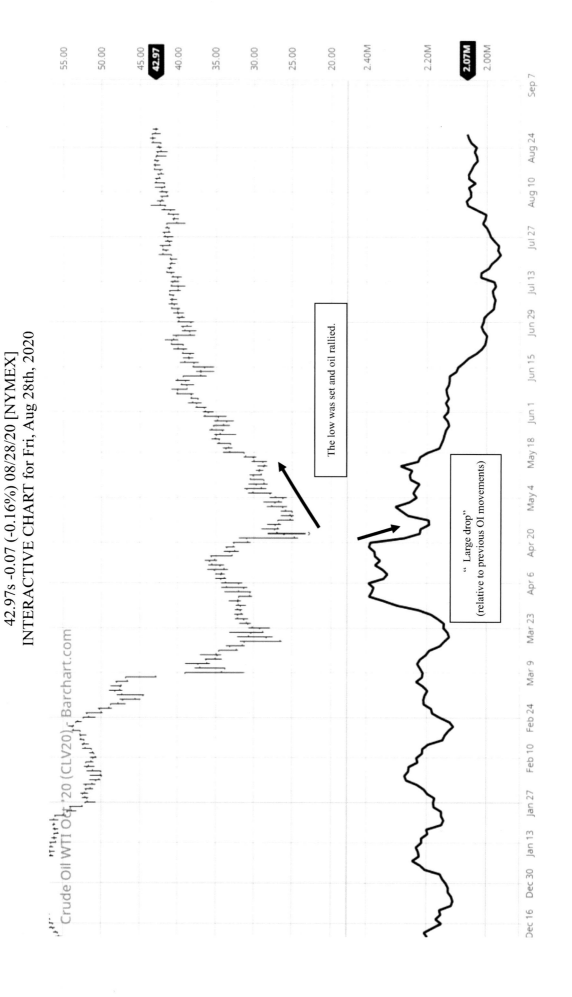

Crude Oil WTI Oct '20 (CLV20)
42.97s -0.07 (-0.16%) 08/28/20 [NYMEX]
INTERACTIVE CHART for Fri, Aug 28th, 2020

The low was set and oil rallied.

" Large drop"
(relative to previous OI movements)

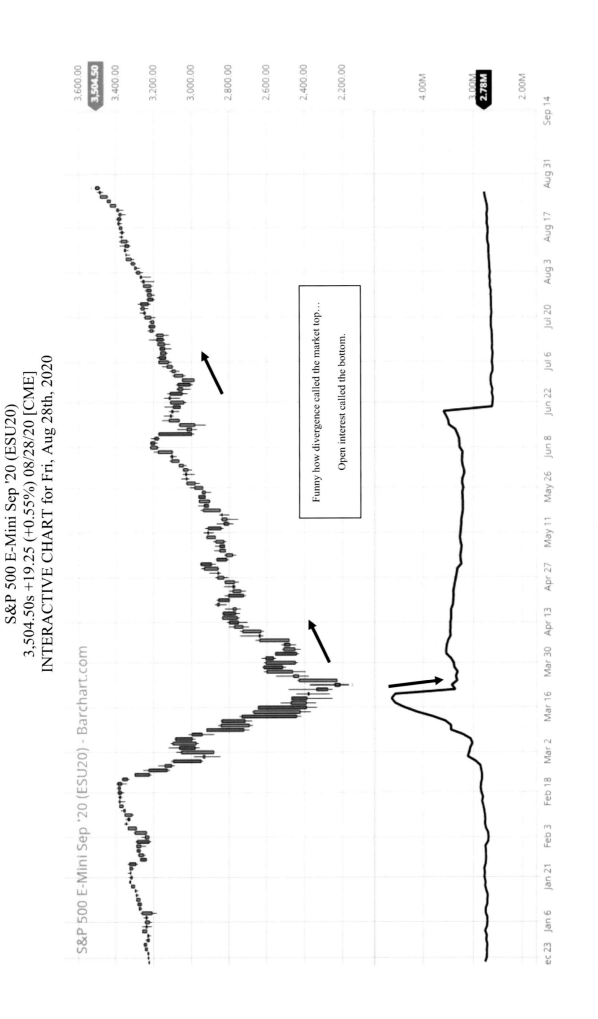

S&P 500 E-Mini Sep '20 (ESU20)
3,504.50s +19.25 (+0.55%) 08/28/20 [CME]
INTERACTIVE CHART for Fri, Aug 28th, 2020

Funny how divergence called the market top.…

Open interest called the bottom.

69

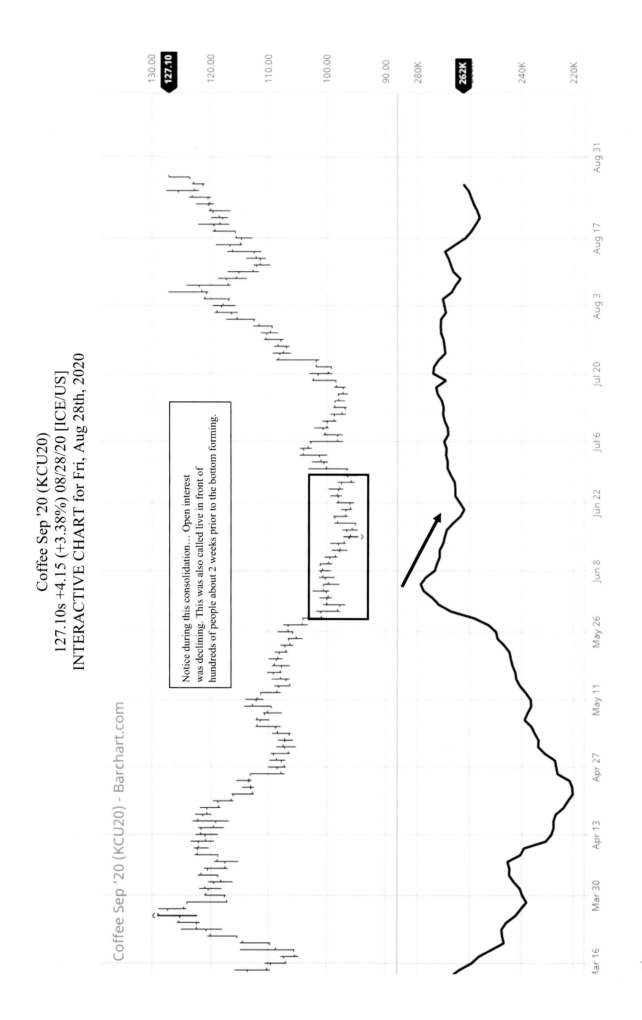

Coffee Sep '20 (KCU20)
127.10s +4.15 (+3.38%) 08/28/20 [ICE/US]
INTERACTIVE CHART for Fri, Aug 28th, 2020

Notice during this consolidation… Open interest was declining. This was also called live in front of hundreds of people about 2 weeks prior to the bottom forming.

Coffee Sep '20 (KCU20) - Barchart.com

70

British Pound Sep '20 (B6U20)
1.3344s +0.0138 (+1.04%) 08/28/20 [CME]
INTERACTIVE CHART for Fri, Aug 28th, 2020

British Pound Sep '20 (B6U20) - Barchart.com

Final thoughts

Open interest is useful and can set the tone for a new trend, but this is not something I monitor every single day. Sometimes I will take a day trade in the direction of the trend, but it is better to hold these trades for longer periods of time. Long-term trading in the forex market is something I normally do not do, but working on it! Still can be useful for traders to get overall high time frame bias.

References

Barchart.com

Commodity Futures Trading Commission. https://www.cftc.gov/

Ganti, A. (2020, August 01). How Open Interest is Determined.

https://www.investopedia.com/terms/o/openinterest.asp

Williams, Larry R. *How I Made One Million Dollars ... Last Year ... Trading Commodities*. Windsor Books, 1979.

Chapter 7

00's, 20's, 50's, & 80's

Learning Objectives

➢ What are 00's, 20's, 50's, & 80's

➢ Why these numbers are important

Also known as *"whole numbers"* or *"psychological levels,"* are simply price levels that end with 0, 2, 5, or 8. In my preference, the more 0's you have, the better. For example, some 00 numbers would be **1.4000** (GBP/USD), **.7400** (AUD/USD), or **1.2000** (EUR/USD). There are completely different from *Fibonacci levels*, which I personally use for retracements. These 00's, 20's, 50's, and 80's are numbers that are represented in the price itself, which is normally found on the right side of your charts. Many traders spend most of their time looking on the left side of the chart that they forget there is a right side! There is nothing wrong with price history, structure, or other details concerning the trade, but price is also just as important.

In *The Quarters Theory* by Ilian Yotov, there are also Quarter Levels which are described as *"... 1000 PIP Ranges between the Major Whole Numbers in currency exchange rates and divides these ranges into four equal parts, called Large Quarters."* These Quarter Levels are just as useful as the rest of the numbers in this chapter, but can also blend into 50 levels since 25, 50, and 75 are quarter levels in which the 5 is incredibly significant. Let me provide a table for you to review the numbers on the EUR/USD pair.

	EUR/USD
Whole Number (00's)	**1.4000**
80 Levels	*1.3800*
	1.3600
50 Levels	*1.3500*
	1.3400
20 Levels	*1.3200*
Whole Number (00's)	**1.3000**
80 Levels	*1.2800*
	1.2600
Quarter Level (or 50)	**1.2500**
	1.2400
20 Levels	*1.2200*
Whole Number (00's)	**1.2000**
80 Levels	*1.1800*
	1.1600
50 Levels	*1.1500*
	1.1400
20 Levels	*1.1200*
Whole Number (00's)	**1.1000**
80 Levels	*1.0800*
	1.0600
50 Levels	*1.0500*
	1.0400
20 Levels	*1.0200*
Whole Number (00's)	**1.0000**

These levels are significant because you will see that there are price responses around these numbers. The difference in time frame will also have effects on how responsive some levels may be. If you are looking at a monthly, weekly, or daily time frame, price may move past these levels to a certain degree before showing responses in the long run.

Here is a hypothetical example:

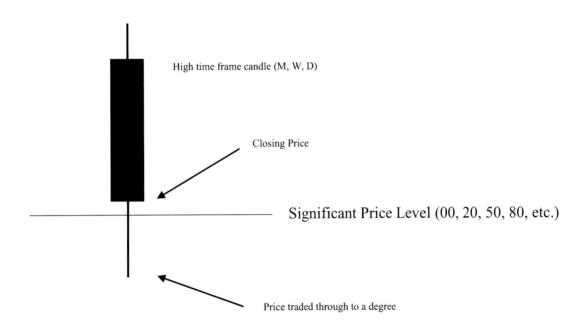

High time frame candle (M, W, D)

Closing Price

Significant Price Level (00, 20, 50, 80, etc.)

Price traded through to a degree

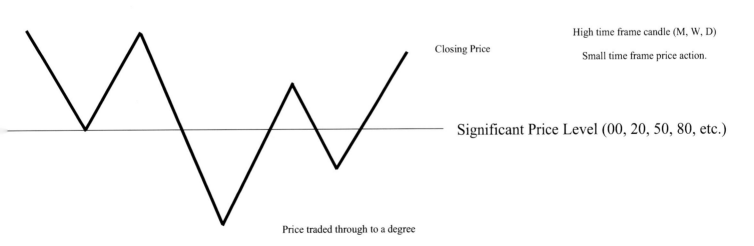

High time frame candle (M, W, D)

Small time frame price action.

Closing Price

Significant Price Level (00, 20, 50, 80, etc.)

Price traded through to a degree

NZD/USD "Kiwi" Daily by Tradingview.com

NZD/USD "Kiwi" 15min by Tradingview.com

AUD/JPY 15min by Tradingview.com

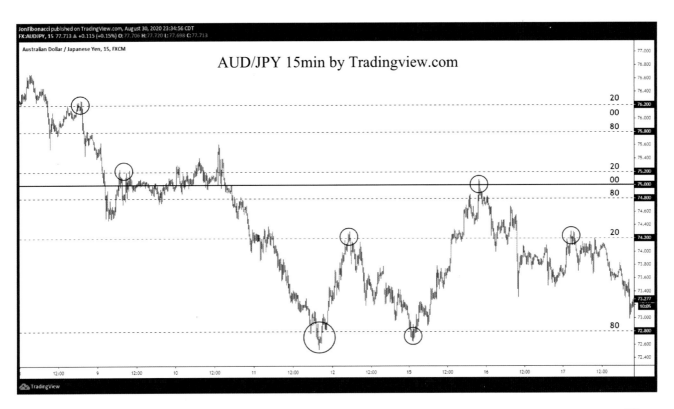

AUD/JPY 15min by Tradingview.com

The way I trade is not just one concept, but rather many concepts blended together. For example, imagine yourself looking for a buying opportunity on a currency pair because you believe the market is going higher in the next couple of days. You can find a concept that is considered high probability and see if a whole number (or 00, 20, or 80) is nearby.

EUR/USD example: Remember the chapter on market manipulation where price would run double bottom and double top formations? Here is one where price was pushed down there and also met an 80 level. This was also something called out to our stream viewers beforehand.

EUR/USD 15min by Tradingview.com

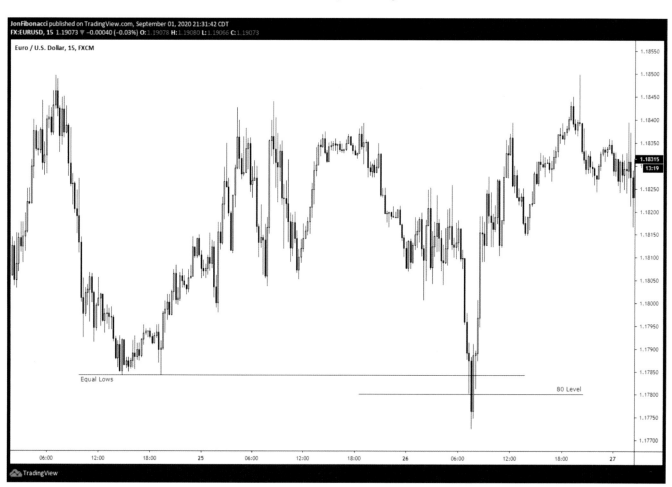

References

Yotov, Ilian. *The Quarters Theory: The Revolutionary New Foreign Currencies Trading Method*. Wiley, 2010.

Chapter 8

Fibonacci Logic

Learning Objectives

➢ Logical use of the Fibonacci retracement tool

➢ Entry Techniques using the Fibonacci retracement tool

Logical use of the Fibonacci retracement tool

Many retail traders believe in supply and demand. They believe the tick-by-tick movements on the screen are created from an excess of supply or an excess of demand. You probably have heard statements such as "more buyers than sellers" or "more sellers than buyers." I think it is not based on the *number* of buyers and sellers, but rather the *volume* of buying or selling. For example, if 100 traders shorted the market with $1.00 of margin, but one trader on the institutional level bought the market with $500 of margin, then the market will increase because the amount of money pumped into the market from long positions outnumbers the amount of money from short sellers. Even though there were more sellers than buyers, price went higher. So instead of thinking about buyers and sellers, it may be a good idea to think about the volume of longs and the volume of shorts.

Who has the *most volume* in the financial markets? It is not retail traders. It is not random people throughout the world who simply open a brokerage account with a few hundred or a few thousand dollars. Your uncle Bob and little Johnny from down the street are not moving markets the same way that smart money moves markets. *"Smart money is the capital that is being controlled by institutional investors, market mavens, central banks, funds, and other financial professionals." (Banton.)* The professionals move price, as well as central banks. After understanding the "who" behind the markets, we can then move forward to "where, when, and why" in later chapters.

Most traders give ambiguous advice to new traders. For example, they will provide information such as "buy low and sell high." Well, duh! The question remains what exactly is high and what exactly is low? High and low can be interpreted in almost an infinite number of ways. One would have to know in which context to use such measurements. As far as the Fibonacci retracement tool, we can use it as a guide to help determine areas of "low" price and areas of "high" price. For those unfamiliar with the Fibonacci retracement tool, it is a tool that measures retracements in the form of percentages. Retracements, normally, are drawn from either a low-to-high manner or high-to-low. There are percentages displayed on the screen (which can be customized and changed) that a trader can look at and consider buying or shorting, and sometimes exiting trades. I am unaware of any charting platform that does not have Fibonacci retracements in their drawing tools repertoire. I personally use *TradingView.com* as my go-to charting service and have been with them for over 5 years as of November 2020.

Retracements above 50% are considered "high" from an overall perspective. Retracements below 50% are considered "low" from an overall perspective. I do not look at any levels prior to the 50%, which is typically displayed on the drawing tool by way of default settings. You may consider going into the tools settings and changing the levels once you are done with this chapter.

My favorite levels are **50%**, **61.8%**, and **78.6%** retracements. Before the 50%, price is too "high" and after 78.6%, price may continue lower (and higher if looking for short positions.) If you dig into your charts and look for examples in hindsight, you may find that the 61.8% level is commonly met for trades that panned out beautifully. This does not mean to only use that level, just that you may come across similar data in your own studies.

Low-to-high drawing for a long position, or buying opportunity

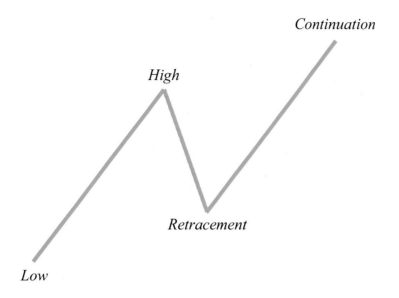

High-to-Low drawing for a Short position, or selling opportunity

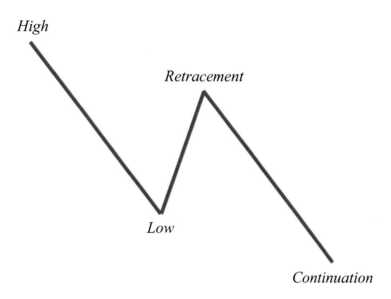

Fibonacci Logic Graphic

"HIGH"

"MEETING IN THE MIDDLE"

"LOW"

Fibonacci Logic Graphic drawn from a low to high (buying a retracement in bullish markets)

50% "Meeting in the middle"

61.8% "Cheap"

78.6% "Cheap"

Fibonacci Logic Chart 1 - Micro E-mini S&P500 Futures (DEC 2020) October 2 - October 13, 2020
Courtesy of Tradingview.com

Notes:

Quick moves in the market can be scary to some investors or traders. In a way, this could be a design to shake out "weak longs." However, those who panic sold their positions probably ended up regretting it later once the market rallied and continued its bullish trend. Price came off a high and slammed right into the "cheap" area at the 61.8% Fibonacci retracement and the 78.6% area. The 78.6% are is exactly where buyers would be getting in a "cheap" price relative to its previous pricing. If I remember this correctly, I think the sharp decline came after the president of the United States tweeted something to social media. The short-term fluctuations do not often last against the major trend. The price action also formed a few weeks after there was a steep decline in open interest, giving potential bullishness.

Fibonacci Logic Chart 2 - Micro E-mini S&P500 Futures (DEC 2020) October 30, 2020
Courtesy of Tradingview.com

The chart above illustrates the price action I was watching that had a lot to do with short

covering. Basically, the idea was that Friday is the end of the week and this was the last week of

the month. Prices had fallen hard throughout the month and I figured smart money was closing

shorts. Remember, closing a short position requires buying back so we anticipated the movement

higher the last 1-2 hours of trading. Spot on!

Fibonacci Logic Chart 3 – AUD/USD 11-11-2020 to 11-12-2020
Courtesy of Tradingview.com

This trade was introduced to our viewers on a live stream, at least 20 minutes or so prior

to the entry. There were additional factors that were added to this analysis like the correlation

divergence with NZD/USD and the combination of a bullish US Dollar Index. However, since

this chapter is on the logical use of Fibonacci retracements, I excluded the additional analysis

and left on the price target near 0.7250, which happens to also be a 50 level.

The Fibonacci price levels above 50% in the case of a shorting opportunity provided

short sellers to get a more favorable price to enter their short positions.

References

Banton, Caroline. "Smart Money." Investopedia, Investopedia, 29 Aug. 2020, www.investopedia.com/terms/s/smart-money.asp.

Chapter 9
EUR/USD, GBP/USD
& EUR/GBP Relationship

We can understand the relationship between EUR/USD and GBP/USD by studying the charts side-by-side or overlapping. These currencies are highly correlated with each other and are inversely correlated with the U.S. Dollar Index or DXY. The movements of these currencies are not always equal in the number of pips or percentage. In certain conditions, one can be experiencing a down day while the other experiences an up day. If these pairs are highly correlated but can still move away from one another, it is a sign of professional *accumulation* or *distribution* (Reference chapter 4).

Professional accumulation or distribution can be found in the breaking away of the correlations. We know this because of how the market operates by way of smart money. Remember, they are the ones who have the power to move price at their will. The understanding of this is what leads to the understanding of future price movements and their characteristics.

EUR/GBP Higher = EUR/USD stronger than GBP/USD

EUR/GBP Lower = EUR/USD weaker than GBP/USD

Conditions:

EUR/GBP Higher = EUR/USD longs in bullish conditions *(bearish DXY)*

EUR/GBP Lower = EUR/USD shorts in bearish conditions *(bullish DXY)*

EUR/GBP Lower = GBP/USD longs in bullish conditions *(bearish DXY)*

EUR/GBP Higher = GBP/USD shorts in bearish conditions *(bullish DXY)*

Divergence:

EUR/GBP Higher = Finding divergence to favor EUR/USD instead of GBP/USD *(bearish DXY)*

➢ *EUR/USD making higher low while GBP/USD makes lower low*

EUR/GBP Lower = EUR/USD shorts in bearish conditions *(bullish DXY)*

➢ *EUR/USD making lower high while GBP/USD makes a higher high*

EUR/GBP Lower = GBP/USD longs in bullish conditions *(bearish DXY)*

➢ *GBP/USD making a higher low while EUR/USD makes a lower low*

EUR/GBP Higher = GBP/USD shorts in bearish conditions *(bullish DXY)*

➢ *GBP/USD making a lower high while EUR/USD makes a higher high*

EUR/GBP EUR/USD and GBP/USD provided by Tradingview.com

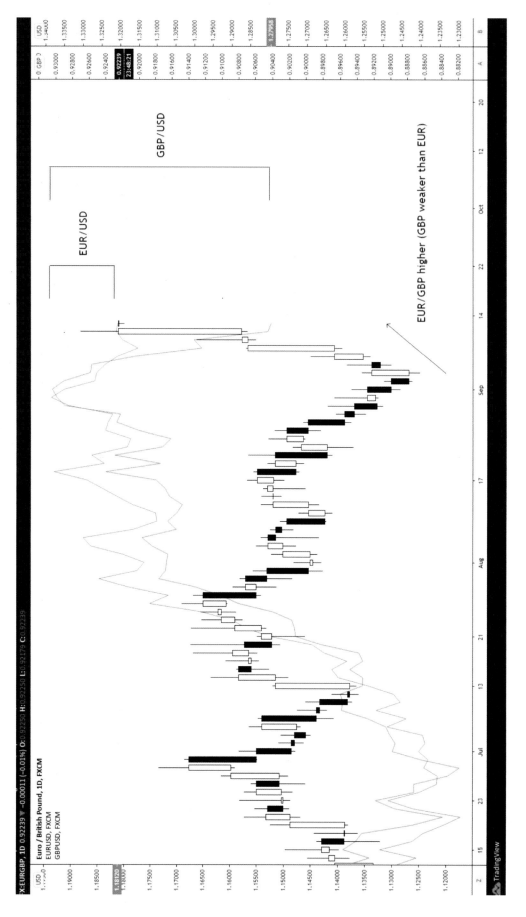

The point of this chart is to indicate that when the currencies retraced lower, since Euro was stronger, GBP fell more pips and percentage to the downside. I look to short weak currency, not strong.

EUR/GBP EUR/USD and GBP/USD provided by Tradingview.com

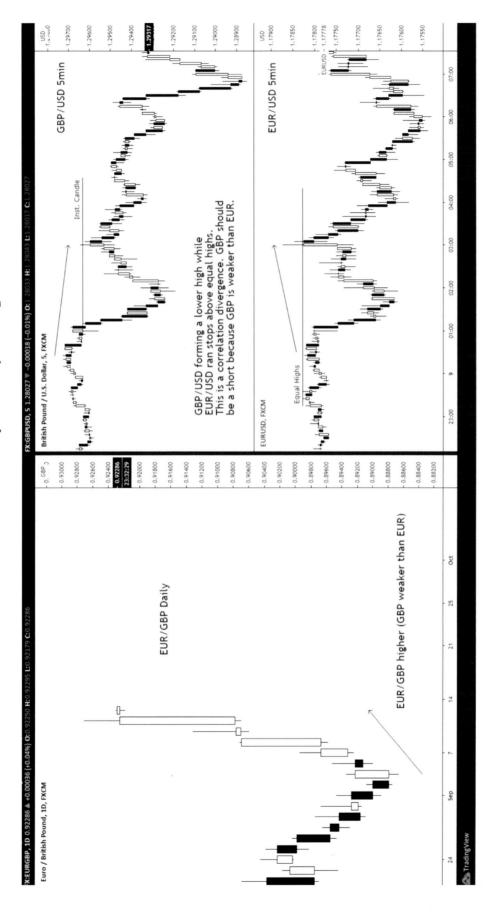

EUR/GBP Higher = GBP/USD shorts in bearish conditions *(bullish DXY)*

➢ *GBP/USD making a lower high while EUR/USD makes a higher high*

EUR/GBP EUR/USD and GBP/USD provided by Tradingview.com

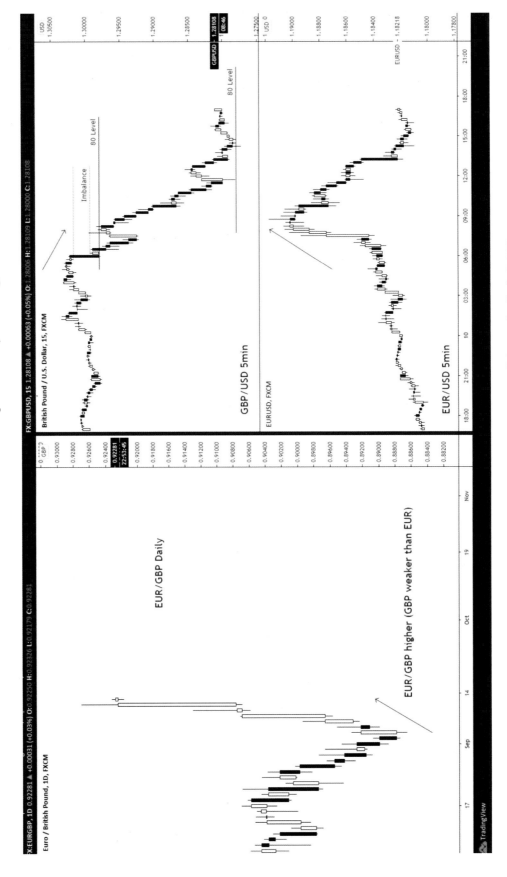

EUR/GBP Higher = GBP/USD shorts in bearish conditions *(bullish DXY)*

➢ *GBP/USD making a lower high while EUR/USD makes a higher high*

Another way of looking at this relationship would be the Libra scale. One side would be EUR/USD (Fiber) and the other side would be GBP/USD (Cable.) The scale itself represents what the cross pair, EUR/GBP, would be. When the scale is tipping to one side, it means the currencies are not equal. One of them is stronger than the other. EUR/GBP has its own chart and does not remain a flat line. This means there are constant shifts in currency strength or weakness. These fluctuations can be used in conjunction with analysis of the individual pairs to get confluence. Essentially, the trader would be stacking the probabilities of a one-sided market. Finding this type of environment can set up for quality trades if analyzed correctly. Below is my *artistic* design of the visual in my head of the scale.

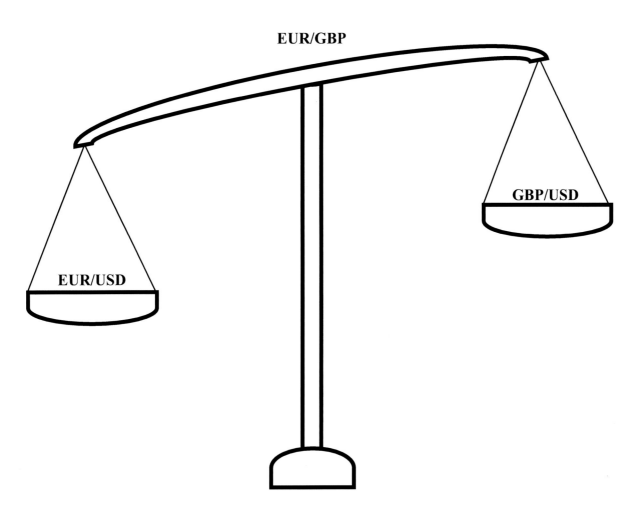

EUR/USD, GBP/USD & EUR/GBP Relationship Final Thoughts

This way of analysis by looking at two, three, or more assets for one trade can be tricky to understand at first. It will take practice and repetition to come to a higher level of understanding. There is nothing wrong with re-reading this chapter, or the entire book, more than once or twice. When I came across this information, I was that way. I needed to study, backtest, and watch price moving forward. I was not an overnight success. As egotistical as some of us may want to be at times, do not forget the market can and will humble you. This information can be easily misinterpreted, and you can (and will) take losing trades.

I have provided a small amount of evidence in this chapter to get your thoughts and curiosity moving. It will be up to you, the reader, the take this information and use it to elevate your knowledge. What you do beyond this read is your responsibility. I can provide the data and analogies, but I cannot force you to understand it.

Chapter 10
The Secret

Hopefully you did not just open my book and flip straight to this page. If you did, shame on you! However, I do not blame you. I probably would have done the same thing. I know what it feels like to look for the answers. For those who went through this the right way, great job for doing it correctly! I think this chapter, the final one, would not be understood or appreciated the same way without first going through the previous nine chapters. Through my 6 ½ years of experience so far (as of November 2020), I have learned the methods to high probability trading, and I have shared many of them in this book. The "secret" is *putting them together in a way that complements one another*. Other traders know this as confluence. When two or more types of analysis tell you the same thing, the odds of winning a trade are considered higher. But this implies that you analyzed the market correctly. If you get it wrong, then chances of a winning trade could be lowered because now the market is doing something other than you thought it would. You could be wrong about the analysis and still be correct on the trade. You may win the trade and look back at what happened and realize you goofed it up but still found yourself a winner. Those scenarios are great because you get to learn and have a winner on the books. Conversely, if you were wrong on the analysis and the trade was a loser, you still get to learn but do not get to mark a winner on the books. I suggest learning from both winners and losers.

Individually, the tools throughout this book are powerful. Together they are supreme and second to nothing (opinion). Now, why would I say this? Of course, I will not just ramble about how good they are without showing you why they are. Many people who have seen me call price action moves 20 minutes, an hour, a few hours, days, weeks, and even months in advance. Some of you may not have so it would be ideal to show the newer people exactly how precise these markets can move. There were some interesting charts I have shown you already. Some were even live trades, and I posted the exact entry and exit. These moves can create real turning points in the markets. My best secret is to stack the probabilities into the favor of the trader.

For the ideal educational content, I have provided chart markups for different types of traders. Some charts will be intraday markups, some will be swing trade related and others long term, or position markups. I do not know *you*. I do not know what type of trader you are. We all have our personalities and way of trading. Some of you will look to day trade while others may want to just take 1-2 trades per month because you want to focus on your current career. For whoever you may be, I hope you find some value in the content provided.

Enjoy.

Intraday Markups

Intraday Chart 1 - AUD/USD 15min, November 6-12, 2020 courtesy of Tradingview.com

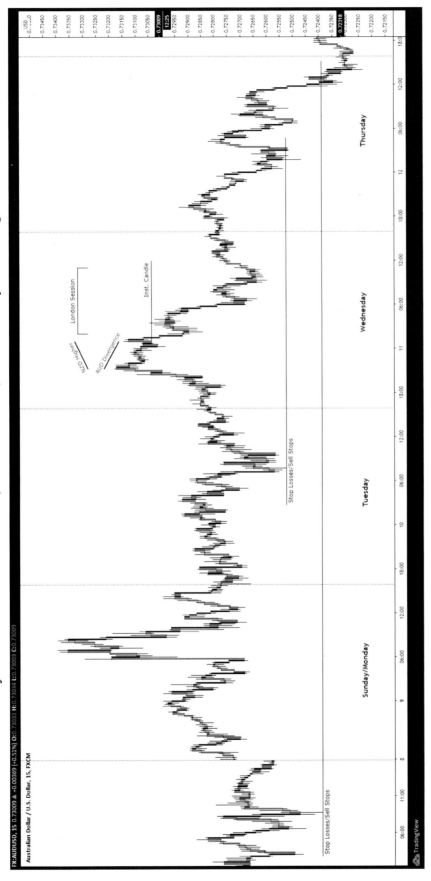

The focus should be on Wednesday. The short opportunity was presented to me through these various techniques. The first was ultimately time and price meaning that we were looking for something to setup during the London session, outlined on the chart. Secondly, we established the Australian dollar was weak by comparing it to its correlating asset, the New Zealand Dollar, also known as NZD or Kiwi. The chart overlay is not marked, but the divergence between the two currencies is annotated with the dark black lines. Kiwi was closing higher while the Aussie was failing to move higher, indicating weakness. Once the weakness was established in the price action, we looked to enter off the 15min Institutional Candle. After the entry was anticipated, we needed a target to the downside which was the potential sell stops resting around price level **.7250** (50 level), which happened to be the low of the previous day on Tuesday. In addition, off the charts, the dollar index was looking to trade higher, which in turn would help pushing Aussie lower. AUD/NZD on the daily was trending lower, further indicating Aussie weakness. I know it sounds like a lot for one trade, but there were less than 2 full pips of drawdown and the market was able to move 50+ pips lower.

Intraday Chart 2 – GBP/USD 15min, November 11, 2020 courtesy of TradingView.com

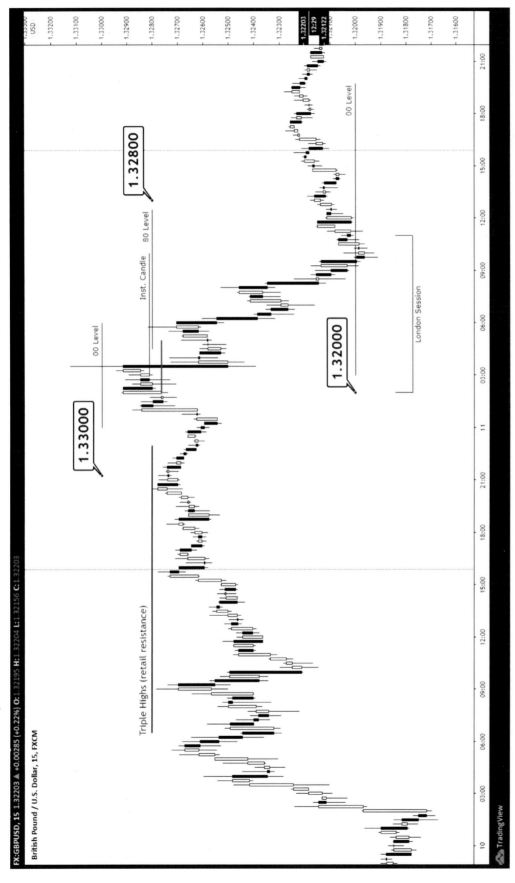

Triple highs are seen as resistance by retail investors. Since the market ran up a little bit past the **1.3300** level and rejected (manipulation), a retracement opportunity was available at the inst. Candle just above **1.3280** (80 level). The red line is indicating the start of the London session and the session's opening price. We would like to see an opportunity to short above the open if we are in bearish market conditions. The market, later in the day, fell down over 80 pips down to the whole number, or 00 level **1.3200** where price then reversed slightly giving short sellers a good trading day near the end of the London session.

101

Intraday Chart 3 – EUR/USD 15min, November 18, 2020

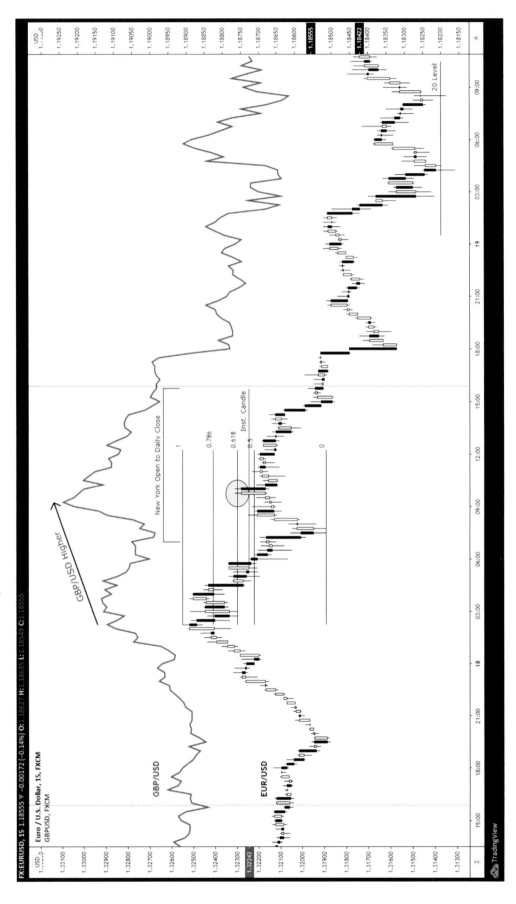

Using the comparison between EUR/USD and GBP/USD, we can clearly identify that EUR/USD is weak because it is failing to make a higher high while GBP/USD is moving higher. Given the displayed weakness, the ideal entry was the **61.8%** Fibonacci retracement. Not just the retracement alone as we also have the level meeting inside of the Inst. Candle which is also inside of the New York session, giving the best time to trade. The highlighted portion is the area to focus on. Notice the " overlap" of 1) Inst. Candle, 2) Fibonacci retracement, and of course, 3) Divergence, which was an opportunity for shorting a weak currency. Price carried its bearishness into the next day and ultimately stopped at the **1.1820** (20 level) area.

Intraday Chart – EUR/USD 5min, October 27, 2020 courtesy of TradingView.com

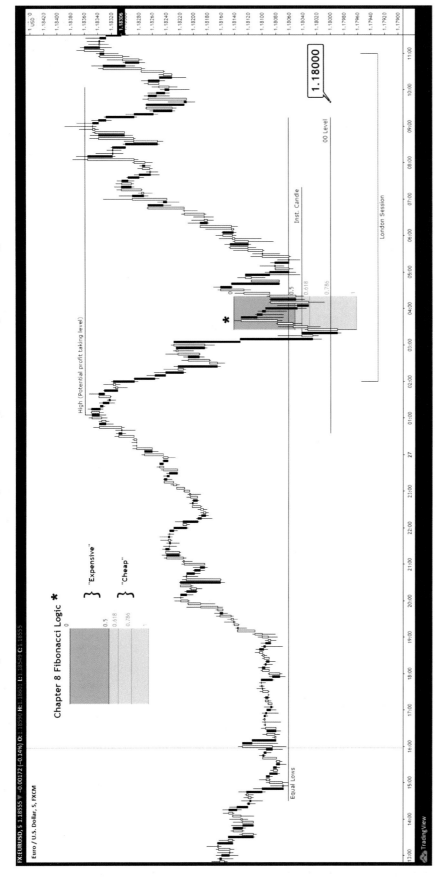

As discussed in Chapter 2 about **market manipulation**, we can clearly see the equal lows (or commonly referred to as a double bottom formation) on the far-left side of the chart. When the market came down, reaching liquidity below those lows, a beautiful buying opportunity showed up shortly after during the London session. After the low was set from the liquidity run, price was able to start trading away from that area. When the market then retraced lower, we can observe an Inst. Candle that happened to also overlap with a **61.8%** Fibonacci retracement for our " cheap" consideration. Price then reached the most recent high, which could also be considered equal highs (small, but still there).

Swing Trade Markups

Swing Trade Chart 1 - USD/CAD November 2020 courtesy of TradingView.com

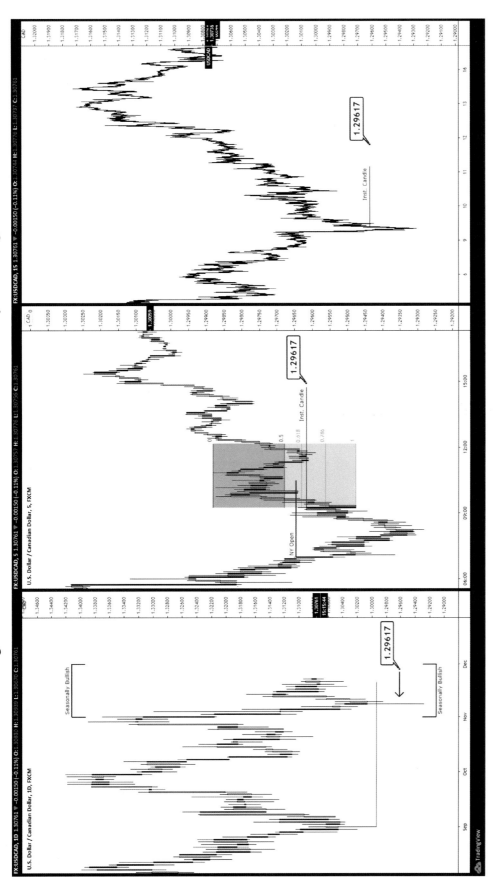

The left chart is Loonie on the Daily time frame. The middle chart is the 5min and the right chart is a 15min zoomed out. Starting from the left, we can see that USD/CAD is seasonally bullish because Canadian Dollar futures are seasonally bearish when looking at seasonal data. I get my seasonal charting data from *Equityclock.com* and use them to spot potential high probability trades if the small time frame trading can align with the seasonal trend. This analysis is also used with higher time frame bias like the open interest. Only I did not write any chapters on seasonality, the information provided here should be enough to get your thoughts rolling. The middle chart (5min) is showing a new high being made and then a retracement is drawn from the most recent low to the most recent high. Then the " cheap" area **61.8%** Fibonacci retracement is in overlap with the Inst. Candle near **1.2962** for the buying opportunity. Small risk, and as seen here, large reward as price then continued higher for a few days.

Swing Trade Chart 2 - Nasdaq & Dow Jones Micro E-Mini futures November 2020 courtesy of TradingView.com

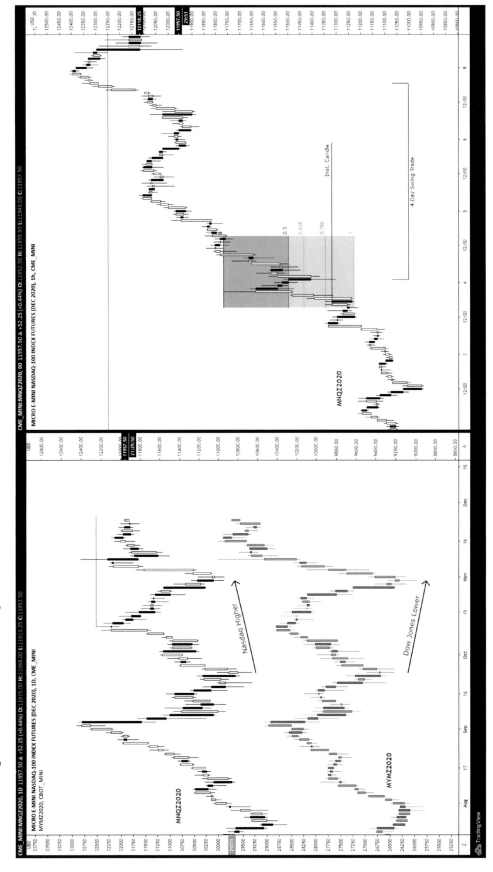

When comparing indices (left chart), we can identify strength in the Nasdaq or Nasdaq stocks that are *outperforming* the benchmark. In this case, I am only viewing the indices and leaving stocks up for you to study on your own. When allowing the low to be set near the start of November, we can start to look for retracements to the downside for long positions. On the right chart, the Inst. Candle is being displayed along with the **78.6%** Fibonacci retracement for the " cheap" price area. Price was then able to rally for a few days and ultimately make a new high where profit taking would be a great idea. Granted this trade only lasted 4 days, if you notice the drawdown compared to the price target, you'll find the risk reward here was very handsome.

Swing Trade Chart 3 – EUR/USD Daily, 5min and 15min September 2020 courtesy of TradingView.com

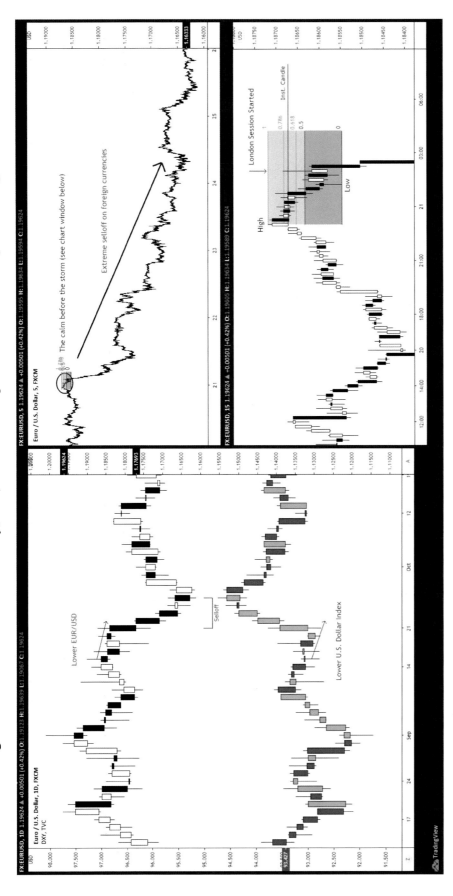

Left Chart: On the daily time frame we can notice a lower dollar index. Now, I start with dollar index and then move to other currencies. So then since the Euro is almost an inverse of the dollar index, Euro should be going higher. However, this chart is telling a different story. The Euro is also going lower, displaying weakness. Traders may want to look for shorting opportunities in weak markets.

Top Right: Notice the extreme selloff on this currency. This move was able to occur for a few days in a row, with minor retracements to the upside.

Bottom Right: The entry technique ideal for this swing trade. We can tell price went to the 78.6% Fibonacci retracement and also overlapping with an Inst. Candle. Additionally, this was the beginning on the London session, an ideal time to look for entering the market.

Swing Trade Chart 4 – AUD/USD 1hr November 2020 courtesy of TradingView.com

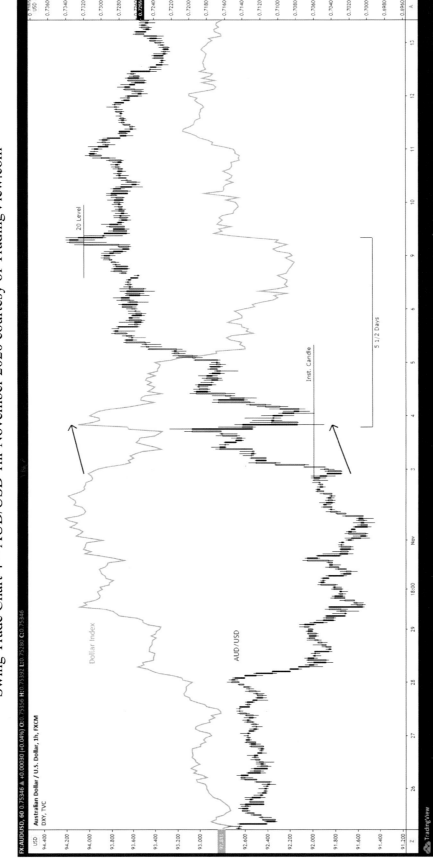

Starting with the Dollar Index, we can identify a higher high with the top arrow. If the Dollar Index is going higher, then it would make sense for the Australian dollar to go lower. However, it is also moving higher which indicates strength. We see Aussie reacting from the institutional candle and rallying for over five days. The top of this move was near the 20 level of .7320 and further proving that 20 levels can be useful if used correctly. I get questions from my mentees about when to enter on a position like this. I would wait for the bottom and then get in on a retracement (not annotated on the above chart).

Position Trade Markups

Position Trade Markups chart 1 – Gold (XAU/USD) Monthly courtesy of TradingView.com

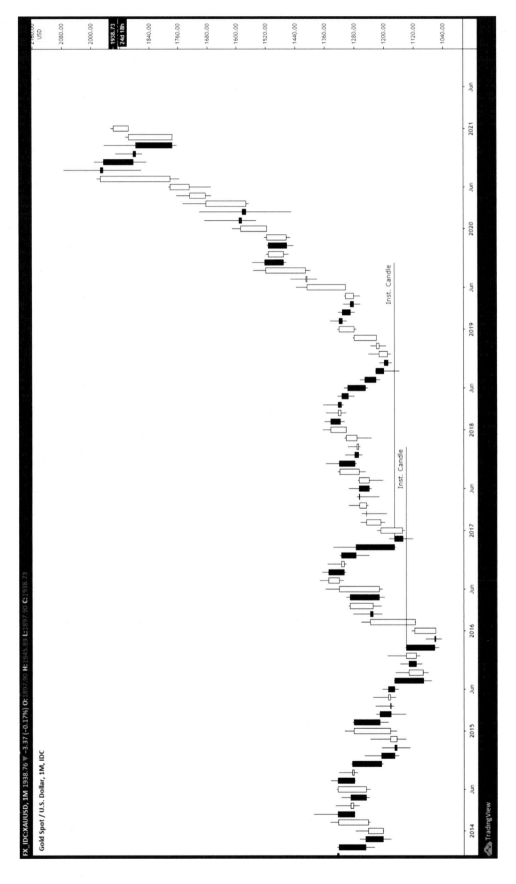

These trades (yes, I took these) were really long term and based on a seasonal pattern for Gold. These trades were not held for as long as they should have been because I was rather impatient. Trust me, lesson well learned.

Position Trade Markups chart 2 – GBP/USD (Cable) and Dollar Index courtesy of TradingView.com

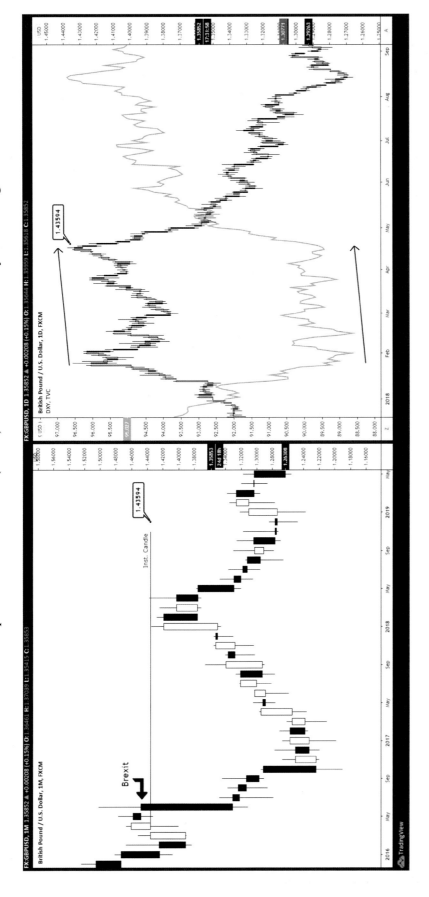

Left: Monthly does have an up candle prior to the aggressive movements lower after the initial Brexit vote in June of 2016. Although I did short the market at the time, another real opportunity presented itself on the return to Brexit pricing.

Right: Daily returns to the Brexit pricing and we see a correlation divergence with the Dollar Index, indicating that the move higher on Cable was just a run on stops. The market then fell over 1,600 pips over the next couple of months.

Position Trade Markups chart 3 – NZD (Kiwi) and AUD (Aussie) Daily November 2020 courtesy of TradingView.com

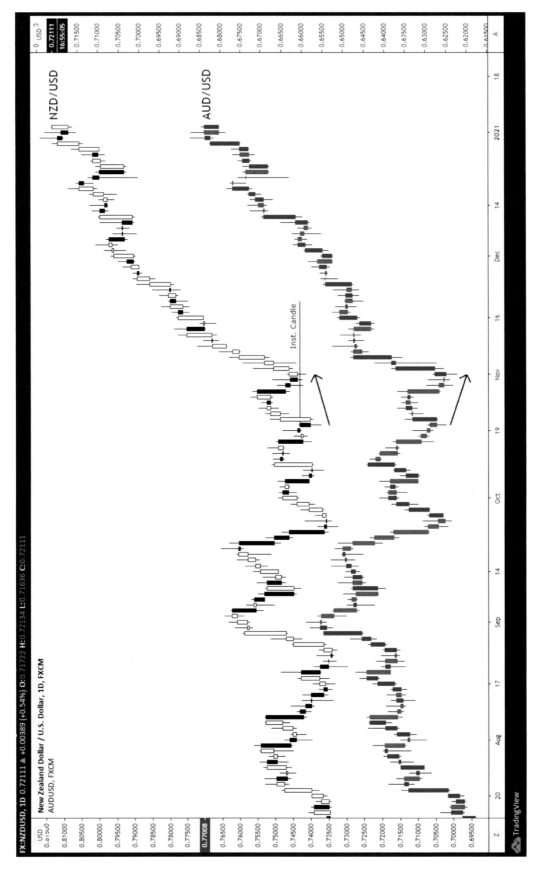

Kiwi (NZD/USD Black & White) we can see outperformance against its correlation, Aussie (AUD/USD Blue & Red) indicating relative strength. When NZD met and respected the daily time frame Inst. Candle, we see a rally of over 550 pips to the upside with only a few down days when compared to the up days in the overall move. Great long term trading opportunities found in these studies. I guess trading does not always have to be too complex.

Position Trade Markups chart 4 – Silver Weekly 2020 courtesy of TradingView.com

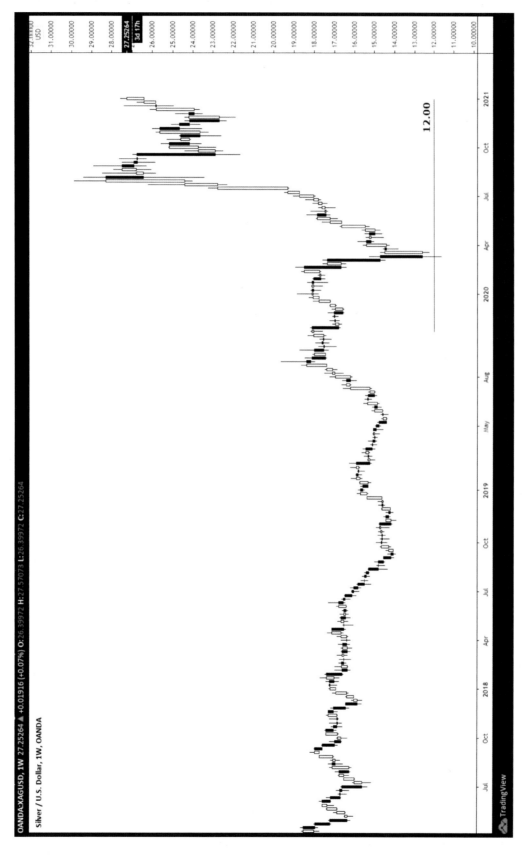

Remember chapter 2?

Final Thoughts & Extras

What I believe about personal development

➤ The majority of your breakthroughs will come from studying on your own. Experience cannot be transferred. You have to work and put in the time. There are no substitutions.

➤ Learn from people who have what you want. Also, learn from the successful and the unsuccessful. You will know what to become and what to avoid becoming. Have multiple mentors, not just one or two.

➤ Stop comparing yourself to others. We are all different people. Some learn faster or slower than others. Do your best and focus on what you need to do. Do not try to become somebody else, but rather the best version of yourself.

➤ Bad days will happen. You will lose a trade, or maybe a job, or get sick because that is just how life works. When you are down, build a plan for getting back on track. Remember if you fail to plan, you plan to fail.

➤ There is so much more to life than money. Enjoy the time with family and friends. Time is our most valuable asset. Grind hard but also live your life. Some people are so poor that all they have is money!

➤ If you need help, ask. Closed mouths do not get fed. Older people have lots of life experience and they will be happy to share their stories and advice with you. There is no need to suffer in silence.

➤ Turn off the television. You are being conditioned and brainwashed. Become an independent thinker! If you go and talk to people you will realize the world is not as bad of a place they make it out to be. Bad news brings more viewers which brings in more advertisement revenue.

➤ Surround yourself with like-minded people. Successful people hang out with other successful people. Losers hang out with other losers. Blood makes you related, but loyalty makes you family. Jim Rohn once stated, *"You are the average of the five people you spend the most time with."*

Five people you should be hanging out with

1) *People who are smarter than you.* You want to gain knowledge from the people who have it. Investing, real estate, health and wellness, finance, or whatever your desire may be. The people who know more than you are the best sources to learn from. You may not spend every moment with these people as they are sometimes hard to come by, but when you are, pay attention. List more than you talk, ask questions, and be thankful.

2) *People who share the same beliefs and values as you.* If you value hard work, then surround yourself and make friends with other hard workers. This will cause all who are involved to operate at a higher level. Teamwork makes the dream work. If you hang around lazy people, you are highly likely to also become lazy.

3) *People who believe in you.* Sometimes we have "off days." The people who believe in you and want to see you succeed will not allow you to fail. These are the people who will give you some motivation or words of encouragement. We all need these types of people in our life. A lot of times we are the ones who need to believe and motivate others.

People do not always believe in themselves and a few moments of encouragement can change their whole day and sometimes can change their whole life.

4) *People who always gave good things to say or nothing at all.* We all know people who are constant complainers. We want to avoid these types of people who bring value to the table or solutions. These are the people who only have problems for every solution. You want to be around the people who say nice things about you when you are not around. These people are the ones who usually can complain but do not. They see the bright side of things. These are amazing people to be around as they can keep the mood in the room positive and away from negative.

5) *People who are fun to be around.* We all need fun in our lives. Sometimes, our friends cannot be businesspeople and our businesspeople cannot be friends. Relieve stress and anxiety by having good times with your friends in a healthy way. Those people who get too drunk to handle themselves are not fun people to be around. The folks who make you laugh until you cry are the ones I am referring to. These people are essential!

What I have learned after 1000 trades

1) *Patience Pays.* I take the most losses on small time frames like the 5-min and 15-min charts. Those trades can set up for extremely high risk-reward trades but unfortunately getting to those home runs can be difficult like experiencing a string of losses. The higher time frames have netted the biggest trades of my career. Holding a winner for weeks or even months in the right direction pays well. Statistically speaking, day traders do not outperform long-term traders. They can, but most do not.

2) *Most traders are terrible at trading* I spent a lot of time studying and watching others who I thought were successful and that is surely not the case majority of the time. I have taken trades based on other people's opinions about the market and most of those trades were losers. Very few trades hit profits. I learned the best route is to become an independent thinker. When I decided to find only the best setups, my results changed.

3) *I have learned to accept that I will be wrong at times.* Nobody sets out to be wrong. Not very many people can truly accept that they will be wrong in trading. I have learned to accept a loss early and that it does not make me a bad trader. It is not always about winning, but sometimes about managing and handling losses. I wish I would have learned this earlier in my career and not have spent so much time chasing perfection. Cutting losses early prevents large equity drawdowns and allows me to focus my attention on finding a better setup or waiting for the next one to present itself. Holding a loser is dumb!

4) *Majority of people have the wrong assumptions about stock markets.* When I was a kid, I thought adults had all the answers. Turns out, most do not know very much about the stock market or investments. The average person will just watch the markets fall and assume that stocks will "come back around." Given the history, as of today, sure, that turned out to be true but who wants to let their retirements take massive drawdown? Most people are also buying stock well after the bull run is over. Dumb money truly does exist.

5) *The markets are absolutely controlled.* Read the books I recommend. This is not something I made up. This is something that is truly learned through observations and exposure to information. I would not be able to call market tops and bottoms if they were not controlled. It still is amazing to watch price do exactly what I want it to do days,

weeks, or even months in advance. Of course, I do not always get it right, but when I am right, it is incredible. Knowing the markets are controlled brings me peace in knowing that trading does not have to be difficult. Invisible hands are at work. I will never meet these people or know who they are, but I know they are out there.

6) *Supply and Demand is a fallacy.* I do not believe supply and demand exist. Remember my earlier comment that most traders are terrible at trading? Most of those folks use S&D techniques and they are losing. What I believe in is finding the trades being controlled by professional traders, also known as "smart money" or "Institutional trading." These are not found in traditional technical analysis. In fact, these players exploit retail analysis. Do not believe me? Do some research and let the charts tell you. It is all in the history.

How to build discipline

1) *Write your goals down daily* or glance at your vision board/whiteboard and remind yourself of why you are doing what you are doing.

2) *Remove Distractions* and surround yourself with like-minded people. End relationships that are not helping you grow and achieve your goals.

3) *Know yourself.* Figure out which time of the day or night you are most productive and then do your best during that time.

4) *Utilize a calendar.* This will let you know what you should be doing. Of course, you should plan things out realistically and do not over-plan your day.

5) *Be healthier.* Eat the right foods, drink water, and develop good sleeping habits. This will allow you to be more productive.

6) *Get an accountability partner or mentor.* If you cannot hold yourself accountable, then find someone to help you stay on track. Do not be afraid to ask for help.

How to manage your time better

1) *Plan tomorrow today.* This will allow you to start the day with momentum.

2) *Set an alarm to wake up or remind yourself of important events.* Use multiple alarms if you are someone like me who is a heavy sleeper!

3) *Leave the house earlier.* Stop arriving late to everything! Everyone notices.

4) *Recognize procrastination.* Just because you are busy does not mean you are getting things done. Avoid endless scrolling through social media.

5) *Avoid distractions.* Limit time-wasting activities like video games. There is a time and place for video games but do not overindulge.

6) *Prioritize.* The captain of my first Navy ship, CDR. Brinn, Neal H., USN, always used to say, "Do the hard things first and everything else becomes easy."

Five things every trader must have

1) *A positive attitude.* Your mindset can make or break your trading. Avoid being gloomy about the learning experiences in trading. Use them to your advantage and learn as much as you can about the markets and yourself. You would be surprised about how much the markets can teach you about life. A negative mind may lead to frustration, anxiety, depression, and usually failure.

2) *Mentors.* Not only for trading but in life as well. You need a leader to hold you accountable and lead the way. Someone that can guide you but not someone spoon-feeding.

3) *Trading journal.* Also can be referred to as a trading workbook, described in *The Complete Trader*, by Paula T. Webb and Mark Douglas. This should include your ideas about the markets, your emotions, etc. One day, when you are years into your journey, you will be glad you documented your experience. You will also have a reference point to measure your growth. How will know how far you have come if you do not know where you started?

4) *Trading Binder.* This one is for printing charts, markups, before-and-after trades, etc. This binder is also something you can study when the markets are not open. Then, when you are ready to pass along knowledge to your family, they will have material that may help shorten their learning curve.

5) *Trading plan.* This is a written and detailed plan on how you are going to approach the markets. When you are going to trade and when you are not going to trade. Which assets you will trade and everything else about a trading plan included.

Example of a trading journal/workbook

Monday August 17, 2020

AUD/NZD pair hitting 1.1000 whole number level. The last time this price was met was almost two years ago so the level should be fresh. If this level will act as a rejection the AUD should diverge against NZD and give AUD weakness. AUD/USD is stuck in a range from .7076 to .7243 and spending majority of the time near the 50% of the range.

Paper trading study: INTC (Intel corp)
     Call Option , $60 Strike price , $1.07 ($107 USD

notes: Huge gap down on the daily time frame. Long term, this stock could see upside back near the 60 price level again.

Tuesday, August 18, 2020

NZD still showing weakness against AUD. 15 min divergence indicated Kiwi lower. Took the short but price did not move "fast" and traded sideways for a few candles. I pulled out near breakeven as it seemed unnecessary to hold the trade.

DXY looking to run daily equal lows.

Shorted AUD/USD @ 7250 after displaying weakness against Kiwi. Price broke the range but look as if to only grab stops above equal highs on 1Hr

Wednesday August 19, 2020

AUD/USD was able to have the anticipated down day but the short at 7250 was a break even trade to avoid a loss or too much drawdown. Price ended up running the previous days high. I think NZD is what propped up AUD as NZD grabbed liquidity above equal highs on the 1hr time frame. Direction was right but the entry was too early. A break even trade is also better than a losing trade.

INTC rallied afterhours from news on a $10B accelerated share repurchase agreements. Up 3-4% afterhours. Thought: Long term, price should trade higher if companies are allowed to buy back their own shares?

Dollar Index ran daily equal lows and reversed, which helped fuel AUD and NZD lower. Low set during London session.

Friday August 21, 2020

AUD/USD sold off until Friday's close, indicating strong selling from anticipated weakness earlier in the week. When Aussie was running previous day liquidity, it diverged against dollar index, giving the indication of manipulation.

In addition, Fiber & Cable diverged at the same time Aussie did but I did not see it until after the fact. Still nice to be able to study.

Monday August 24, 2020

S&P 500 at all-time highs as anticipated over the last several months. Earlier in the year, we noted drastic changes in open interest to help confirm that the bottom was set and that we were ready to head for the daily gap fill and then all-time highs after that. Today we're here.

Dow Jones is lagging behind but looks promising that it also wants to fill its daily gap soon. May look to buy on weakness for a chance to get in before the gap fills.

Prior to the London session, it appears the indices are diverging against one another signifying a weak Nasdaq. Nasdaq failed to make a higher high while the other indices made higher highs. Very clean inst candle on the 15 min time frame post strong selloff. Took the short but exited a few hours later as price stayed flat until London opened. Will follow up in tomorrow's session to see how price panned out.

Tuesday August 25, 2020

Cable daily timeframe signifies that the yields are diverging for a buy signal. 17th low to 21st low on the line chart are going lower on the 5 & 10 year yields while the 30 year yield is going higher. Cable swept last weeks low and has reversed higher. There are equal lows on the 1 hr that are also below the daily open. Looking to buy below the equal lows and targeting higher pricing

5

10

30

123

Wednesday, August 26, 2020

Dow Jones looks good for long positions to head for the daily gap fill. The other indices have already done that and more. I think Dow should be next in line. The Nasdaq is continuing to make new highs and so is the S&P. Looking to take a long position below the daily open for a potential bullish day. Risking small capital for much larger gain. This time around I have taken 2 contracts instead of just 1. Looking to book profits on one and to hold the other long term. I need to check with the broker to see if they will roll the contract over or close me out manually. If the trade pans out I will call them tomorrow and get it figured out and noted for later trades. New York should be providing better movement for the indices but I am going to sleep. If the trade is a loser, I will look to go long again at another time.

2PM - Dow stopped out with small loss. I moved the stop to reduce risk before going to bed and was taken out.

British Pound - Entry missed by 5 pips

Thursday August 27, 2020

Stayed up way too late and was too tired to journal beforehand
so I'll update now. Was taking a look at Cable still, even
though we missed a trade earlier this week. Thursday is a
completely new trading day and I focused on findin a good
setup. Still looking for long positions as the original target
had not been met yet. Yesterday during Cable's run higher,
it left an imbalance on the 1 hour and 15min (inside 1hr)
which also aligned past the 50% fib retracement. Put the order
in and went to bed. Woke up to 110 pips banked. Exited
at the almost high of the day after an entry almost at
the low of the day.

Fiber had a similar setup but cable seemed more likely
to be more bullish.

Dollar index spiked lower as well taking liquidity and
rebalancing price. Todays news was Fed chair Powell speaking
after 8am and Jackson Hole Symposium which I believe
were the excuses to manipulate price.

The indices all went higher but took no trade. After today's
trade, I am done for the week.

The trade binder is an easy enough idea to understand without the need for examples here. Mark up your own charts and print them out. It is that easy! A trading plan I cannot give you either as you must build your own throughout your career as a trader. It can change at times so there is no one-size-fits-all trade plan I can give you. What has been provided to you so far should be enough to kick-start the rest of your journey!

May you do your best, always.

A Letter to the
Young Struggling Trader

Hey friend,

So you have recently started your trading journey. Congratulations! Maybe you have been around for a while but need a little bit more to get to the next level in your trading. Well, I will have you know that we all started somewhere. We all have beginnings and our struggling periods before we can become great. It is only natural to go through a learning curve. For a few, it can be longer or shorter than others. I want to reach out and give you encouragement that could potentially help you along your journey.

You may face many psychological battles throughout your career as a trader. You may think of thoughts such as wishing you should have held winning traders longer. Possibly, you may think that you should have cut your losses earlier than you did. You may question why you moved your stop loss further away as price moved towards your stop. You may look around at everyone else and it seems as if others are trading successfully and you are the only one struggling. This type of thinking is most likely going to hinder your performance as a trader. Other people usually only post winning trades and avoid posting their losers. Active traders that only take winning trades do not exist. There are other people struggling just as you are and just as I once did and sometimes still do. Keep your focus on yourself and your development as a trader. Do not worry about what everyone else is doing. Let other people do what they want to do.

Believe that you can achieve the skillset of trading. The first beginning to the path of success starts with your attitude. If you think you can learn to trade, then you can learn to trade. If you think trading is too hard, then yes, it is too hard. I suggest avoiding toxic environments such as trading chat rooms, telegram groups, discord channels, forums, or other social media mediums. Other people are in search of the answers just as you are and they most likely will not be found on social media.

I would also suggest journaling your trades, your emotions, beliefs about the market, and the charts. This way you can identify mistakes and potentially fix them moving forward. You will not know how far you have come without first knowing where you were. It may not seem beneficial in the short run, but it will be in the long run. In addition to that, a trading plan is essential. A written, well thought out trading plan. A methodology that you create for yourself that is tailored to your experience and personality. Everyone needs a roadmap or set of rules to follow if they want the highest probability for success.

You can do this… but only if you want to.

Frequently Asked Questions

How long will it take me to become a profitable trader?

I do not promise that anyone will become profitable. Out of the traders who do become profitable, from what I have witnessed over the years, the time it takes is different for each person. Not everyone becomes a profitable trader.

Do you have a set percentage you pull profits in a given day?

No set percentage. I do like trading with a risk reward-ratio of 1:3 minimum. If I can get a couple of good trades in and secure the bag, then there is no reason to keep going. I like to be done by Wednesday or Thursday close of business. If you set a goal too high, you may feel discouraged or frustrated if you do not meet it. That could affect your trading in the future.

How many pairs should we be focusing on when sticking to the 2-hour and 4-hour time frame?

That is going to be different for everybody. If you are new to trading, maybe try 2 or 3. If you are a seasoned vet, you may be able to look at more. No need to rush building up a watch list. Move at your own pace. Whatever you are comfortable with.

How often are you looking at charts? Mark up, evaluate the move, and do you set alerts?

I look at charts a lot. Like… a lot. I do not really set alerts. I do not utilize price alerts anymore. I would rather set a pending limit order and let it do what it does.

What checklist would you recommend to someone who is about to commit to forex?

Good question! Get a binder, page protectors, notebooks, pens, and whatever else you need to take notes with. Be prepared to also set aside time to study trading. Be coachable and open-minded.

What account size do you recommend to start trading NASDAQ, Dow Jones, and S&P500?

Depends on what broker you use. For a regulated futures broker, I would not start my account with less than $5,000 USD. Unregulated brokers will probably let you trade with $100 or something small like that but I do not recommend doing anything with the minimum. That is my personal opinion. Check your broker's margin requirements and go from there.

What is your signature trade?

The trade that comes when you are in the "zone" and do not even need to think. Almost like you just know it will be a winner. Usually comes from combining 2 or more concepts (outlined in this book). You just "feel it."

What are the best pairs to start trading?

The majors. Once you understand those, get into correlations.

How did you train yourself to have the indifference needed to the outcome of any trade?

The outcome of any trade could win, lose, or break even. That is just something I understand. That is also something Mark Douglas teaches which is why I recommend reading his material. You either learn the reality or do not. You will lose trades. They will not always be winners.

What got you into trading and why?

Pure curiosity at a young age. Nobody ever talked about it, either, except for my dad. Ultimately, I had to do my own research. Then once I found out that you can put money in and potentially get more money out, I was intrigued. Hooked after my first trade (and a very profitable one, too.)

Can someone turn $50 to $1M in forex?

Probably could. Not saying it is impossible, but the chances are slim. I would not attempt it.

Can a $50k - $100k income be made from trading alone?

Yes.

Do you use any indicators when marking up a chart?

No.

How do you deal with your emotions when having a bad day/week in the markets?

Food! (kidding.) We will not be perfect and there will always be more opportunities in the future. This is why it is a good idea to keep losses small.

Did you ever go through a burst cycle where you would make a certain percentage then lose it?

Yes, when I was a beginner. Now, I manage risk and expectations. No need for wild equity curves.

Do you trade VIX?

I monitor the VIX. Trading that comes with around a $13,000 margin requirement and though I have enough funds to trade it, I do not. I have spoken about VIX for years. Never traded it.

How important are Fibonacci levels?

Fibonacci levels are simple math. I do not believe they hold a lot of weight in technical analysis, but they do play a role. I personally do not use levels prior to the 50% retracement. I prefer the

61.8% and 78.6% levels majority of the time. They are not always a requirement for me to enter a trade.

How do I change my emotional relationship to money?

That is a hard one. I guess it is all about perception. For me, I understand that money is not even real. It is just a means of exchange. No amount can make anyone happy and there is an infinite amount of it because it can be printed and devalued at any time. We grew up being conditioned that money was/is valuable, but I do not personally believe it is as important as most people make it out to be.

What would be a question to ask what you enjoy answering and wish people would ask more?

How I got started. It reminds me of my dad the stories he would tell me about my grandpa buying and selling stock. My grandpa (both from my mom's side and dad's side) died when I was too young to remember them. I know one traded stock and getting asked about how I got started sort of hits home.

Does success change people or reveal their true personality?

Probably both. I do not really think people change in the long run. Some do. Some do not. We are humans. We act like trash, especially when having a lot of money/success. There are good wealthy people and successful people, but I do not know. Celebrities and lottery winners tend to crash and burn. That says a lot. Humans are sinful by nature. That is just reality and some people cannot control their sinful impulses. Some control them better than others. Overall hard to say. Trust me, ego is a monster.

What was your biggest breakthrough with trading?

That everything is controlled and manipulated. Single-handedly my biggest breakthrough of all time. When it finally clicked, I smiled for a long time.

In your personal experience what has helped keep you consistent in what you do?

On word. It applies to anything. To stay consistent to stay motivated and driven, to be completely relentless in your pursuit is to be one word. Passionate.

What is your opinion on trading just a few assets versus trading a lot of them?

If you saw ten $100 bills on the ground, would you pick up just one? Maybe two or three? Would you pick up five? Would seven be enough? Or are you going to pick up all ten and move along? I am the type of person to pick up all ten because it makes the most sense. Someone telling me to focus on two to three assets is like only picking up two to three $100 bills and leaving the other seven to blow away in the wind. That is just dumb. In other words, I believe a person has limited themselves from potential additional opportunities.

Your greatest doubt and how you conquer it?

I do not know about doubt, but my greatest fear is complacency. That is what I want to keep reading, trading, and growing in all aspects to avoid it.

Who introduced you to smart money?

Sam Seiden on YouTube. He was talking about his time on the trading floors and seeing the orders of large banks and institutions. I found it pretty unique and wanted to be on the same side the banks were. Really just took off from there. I am a little shocked "smart money" is not as popular as it should be. Larry Williams and George Angell were writing about this stuff in the '70s and '80s but not very many people seem to know about it.

Do you care more about account percentage or how many quality setups you can get?

#1 is account preservation and #2 is risk management. But to answer your question more directly, I would care more about percentages. The number of trades does not really matter. Do not let these social media traders fool you.

What is your best decision that you ever made in trading?

Studying seasonality and a little bit of economics. Makes the long-term moves more understandable and that is where the big money is.

What is the #1 advice you would give a newbie?

Relax. Enjoy the process. Do not rush. Ask questions. Study hard. Read. Do not focus on anyone else's results but your own.

How do you challenge your emotions?

Emotions are part of being human. There is no problem having them. However, trading based on those emotions can hinder your success as a trader. Plan the trade and trade the plan.

Glossary

Courtesy of Investopedia.com

Asset – A financial asset is a liquid asset that gets its value from a contractual right or ownership claim. Cash, stocks, bonds, mutual funds, and bank deposits are all are examples of financial assets. Unlike land, property, commodities, or other tangible physical assets, financial assets do not necessarily have inherent physical worth or even a physical form. Rather, their value reflects factors of supply and demand in the marketplace in which they trade, as well as the degree of risk they carry. (https://www.investopedia.com/terms/f/financialasset.asp)

B

Backtesting – allows a trader to simulate a trading strategy using historical data to generate results and analyze risk and profitability before risking any actual capital. A well-conducted backtest that yields positive results assures traders that the strategy is fundamentally sound and is likely to yield profits when implemented in reality. A well-conducted backtest that yields suboptimal results will prompt traders to alter or reject the strategy. Particularly complicated trading strategies, such as strategies implemented by automated trading systems, rely heavily on backtesting to prove their worth, as they are too arcane to evaluate otherwise. (https://www.investopedia.com/terms/b/backtesting.asp)

Bearish/Bear Market – A market in which price is declining.

Base Currency – In the forex market, currency unit prices are quoted as currency pairs. The base currency – also called the transaction currency - is the first currency appearing in a currency pair quotation, followed by the second part of the quotation, called the quote currency or the counter currency. In forex, the base currency represents how much of the quote currency is needed for you to get one unit of the base currency. For example, if you were looking at the CAD/USD currency pair, the Canadian dollar would be the base currency and the U.S. dollar would be the quote currency. (https://www.investopedia.com/terms/b/basecurrency.asp)

Bear Trap – A bear trap denotes a technical pattern that occurs when the performance of a stock, index or other financial instrument incorrectly signals a reversal of a rising price trend. A bull trap denotes the opposite of this phenomenon, in which the reversal of a declining trend is falsely signaled. A bear trap can prompt a market participant to expect a decline in the value of a financial instrument, prompting the execution of a short position on the asset.

(https://www.investopedia.com/terms/b/beartrap.asp)

Bid and Ask – The term bid and ask (also known as bid and offer) refers to a two-way price quotation that indicates the best price at which a security can be sold and bought at a given point in time. The bid price represents the maximum price that a buyer is willing to pay for a security. The ask price represents the minimum price that a seller is willing to receive. A trade or transaction occurs after the buyer and seller agree on a price for the security. The difference between bid and ask prices, or the spread, is a key indicator of the liquidity of the asset. In general, the smaller the spread, the better the liquidity. (https://www.investopedia.com/terms/b/bid-and-ask.asp)

Blue Chip – A blue chip is a nationally recognized, well-established, and financially sound company. Blue chips generally sell high-quality, widely accepted products and services. Blue chip companies are known to weather downturns and operate profitably in the face of adverse economic conditions, which helps to contribute to their long record of stable and reliable growth.

The name "blue chip" came about from the game of poker in which the blue chips have the highest value. (https://www.investopedia.com/terms/b/bluechip.asp)

Bond Yield – Bond yield is the return an investor realizes on a bond. The bond yield can be defined in different ways. Setting the bond yield equal to its coupon rate is the simplest definition. The current yield is a function of the bond's price and its coupon or interest payment, which will be more accurate than the coupon yield if the price of the bond is different than its face value. More complex calculations of a bond's yield will account for the time value of money and compounding interest payments. These calculations include yield to maturity (YTM), bond equivalent yield (BEY) and effective annual yield (EAY). (Discover the difference between Bond Yield Rate vs. Coupon Rate).

Bond Yield Vs. Price

As bond prices increase, bond yields fall. For example, assume an investor purchases a bond that matures in five years with a 10% annual coupon rate and a face value of $1,000. Each year, the bond pays 10%, or $100, in interest. Its coupon rate is the interest divided by its par value. (https://www.investopedia.com/terms/b/bond-yield.asp)

Bull / Bullish – A bull is an investor who thinks the market, a specific security or an industry is poised to rise. Investors who adopt a bull approach purchase securities under the assumption that they can sell them later at a higher price. Bulls are optimistic investors who are attempting to profit from the upward movement of stocks, with certain strategies suited to that theory. (https://www.investopedia.com/terms/b/bull.asp)

Bull Trap – A bull trap is a false signal, referring to a declining trend in a stock, index or other security that reverses after a convincing rally and breaks a prior support level. The move "traps" traders or investors that acted on the buy signal and generates losses on resulting long positions. A bull trap may also refer to a whipsaw pattern. *What Does a Bull Trap Tell You?* A bull trap occurs when a trader or investor buys a security that breaks out above a resistance level - a common technical analysis-based strategy. While many breakouts are followed by strong moves higher, the security may quickly reverse direction. These are known as "bull traps" because traders and investors who bought the breakout are "trapped" in the trade. (https://www.investopedia.com/terms/b/bulltrap.asp)

C

Candlestick – A candlestick is a type of price chart used that displays the high, low, open, and closing prices of a security for a specific period. It originated from Japanese rice merchants and traders to track market prices and daily momentum hundreds of years before becoming popularized in the United States. The wide part of the candlestick is called the "real body" and tells investors whether the closing price was higher or lower than the opening price (black/red if the stock closed lower, white/green if the stock closed higher). (https://www.investopedia.com/terms/c/candlestick.asp)

Correlation – Correlation, in the finance and investment industries, is a statistic that measures the degree to which two securities move in relation to each other. Correlations are used in advanced portfolio management, computed as the correlation coefficient, which has a value that must fall between -1.0 and +1.0. (AUD/USD & NZD/USD are a correlation) (https://www.investopedia.com/terms/c/correlation.asp)

Commodity – A commodity is a basic good used in commerce that is interchangeable with other commodities of the same type. Commodities are most often used as inputs in the production of other goods or services. The quality of a given commodity may differ slightly, but it is essentially uniform across producers. When they are traded on an exchange, commodities must also meet specified minimum standards, also known as a basis grade. They tend to change rapidly from year to year. Examples: Gold (XAU/USD) Silver (XAG/USD) USOIL, Copper, etc. (https://www.investopedia.com/terms/c/commodity.asp)

Currency Swap – A currency swap, sometimes referred to as a cross-currency swap, involves the exchange of interest – and sometimes of principal – in one currency for the same in another currency. Interest payments are exchanged at fixed dates through the life of the contract. It is a foreign exchange transaction and is not required by law to be shown on a company's balance sheet. (https://www.investopedia.com/terms/c/currencyswap.asp)

D

Dark Pool – A dark pool is a private financial forum or exchange for trading securities. Dark pools allow investors to trade without exposure until after the trade has been executed. Dark pools are a type of alternative trading system that give investors the opportunity to place orders and make trades without publicly revealing their intentions during the search for a buyer or seller. Dark pools emerged in the 1980s when the Securities and Exchange Commission (SEC) allowed brokers to transact large blocks of shares. Electronic trading and an SEC ruling in 2007 that was designed to increase competition and cut transaction costs have stimulated an increase in the number of dark pools. Dark pools can charge lower fees than exchanges because they are often housed within a large firm and not necessarily a bank. (https://www.investopedia.com/terms/d/dark-pool.asp)

Day Trader – A day trader is a trader who executes a large volume of short and long trades to capitalize on intraday market price action. The price action is a result of temporary supply and demand inefficiencies caused due to purchases and sales of the asset. (https://www.investopedia.com/terms/d/daytrader.asp)

Double Bottom – A double bottom pattern is a technical analysis charting pattern that describes a change in trend and a momentum reversal from prior leading price action. It describes the drop of a stock or index, a rebound, another drop to the same or similar level as the original drop, and finally another rebound. The double bottom looks like the letter "W". The twice-touched low is considered a support level. (This is one of the patterns we expect smart money to exploit and we try to align ourselves with) (https://www.investopedia.com/terms/d/doublebottom.asp)

Double Top – A double top is an extremely bearish technical reversal pattern that forms after an asset reaches a high price two consecutive times with a moderate decline between the two highs. It is confirmed once the asset's price falls below a support level equal to the low between the two prior highs. (This is one of the patterns we expect smart money to exploit and we try to align ourselves with) (https://www.investopedia.com/terms/d/doubletop.asp)

Dow Jones – The Dow Jones Industrial Average (DJIA) is an index that tracks 30 large, publicly-owned companies trading on the New York Stock Exchange (NYSE) and the NASDAQ. The Dow Jones is named after Charles Dow, who created it in 1896, and his business partner, Edward Jones. Often referred to as "the Dow," the DJIA is one of the oldest, single most-watched indices in the world. To investors, the Dow Jones is defined as a collection of blue-chip companies with consistently stable earnings that include Walt Disney Company, Exxon Mobil Corporation, and Microsoft Corporation. When the TV networks say "the market is up today," they are generally referring to the Dow. (https://www.investopedia.com/terms/d/djia.asp)

Downtrend – A downtrend refers to the price action of a security that moves lower in price as it fluctuates over time. While the price may move intermittently higher or lower, downtrends are characterized by lower peaks and lower troughs over time. Technical analysts pay attention to downtrends because they represent something more than a random losing streak. Securities in a downtrend seem to be more likely to continue trending lower until some market condition changes, implying that a downtrend marks a fundamentally deteriorating condition. A downtrend can be contrasted with an uptrend. (https://www.investopedia.com/terms/d/downtrend.asp)

E

Equilibrium – The state in which market supply and demand balance each other, and as a result, prices become stable. Generally, an over-supply of goods or services causes prices to go down, which results in higher demand. The balancing effect of supply and demand results in a state of equilibrium. (https://www.investopedia.com/terms/e/equilibrium.asp)

F

Fair Value – Fair value is a term with several meanings in the financial world. In investing, it refers to an asset's sale price agreed upon by a willing buyer and seller, assuming both parties are knowledgeable and enter the transaction freely. For example, securities have a fair value that is determined by a market where they are traded. In accounting, fair value represents the estimated worth of various assets and liabilities that must be listed on a company's books. (https://www.investopedia.com/terms/f/fairvalue.asp)

Fibonacci Retracement – A Fibonacci retracement is a term used in technical analysis that refers to areas of support or resistance. Fibonacci retracement levels use horizontal lines to indicate where possible support and resistance levels are. Each level is associated with a percentage. The percentage is how much of a prior move the price has retraced. The Fibonacci retracement levels are 23.6%, 38.2%, 61.8% and 78.6%. While not officially a Fibonacci ratio, 50% is also used. The indicator is useful because it can be drawn between any two significant price points, such as a high and a low, and then the indicator will create the levels between those two points. (Personally, I use 50% 61.8% 78.6% and 88.6% and nothing below 50%. I like to think in terms of "sale price." For example, an asset is 78.6% off from the high which may be a good buying opportunity to purchase an asset at a sale) (https://www.investopedia.com/terms/f/fibonaccilines.asp)

Foreign Exchange (Forex) – Foreign Exchange (forex or FX) is the trading of one currency for another. For example, one can swap the U.S. dollar for the euro. Foreign exchange transactions can take place on the foreign exchange market, also known as the Forex Market. The forex market is the largest, most liquid market in the world, with trillions of dollars changing hands every day. There is no centralized location, rather the forex market is an electronic network of banks, brokers, institutions, and individual traders (mostly trading through brokers or banks). (https://www.investopedia.com/terms/f/foreign-exchange.asp)

Futures – are derivative financial contracts that obligate the parties to transact an asset at a predetermined future date and price. Here, the buyer must purchase, or the seller must sell the underlying asset at the set price, regardless of the current market price at the expiration date. Underlying assets include physical commodities or other financial instruments. Futures contracts detail the quantity of the underlying asset and are standardized to facilitate trading on a futures exchange. Futures can be used for hedging or trade speculation. (https://www.investopedia.com/terms/f/futures.asp)

G

Gap – is an area of a chart where a security's price either rises or falls from the previous day's close with no trading occurring in between. (https://www.investopedia.com/terms/g/gap.asp)

GBP – Referred to as British Pound Sterling or simply "British Pound" or "Pound." GBP/USD is a major currency pair which holds the nickname "Cable." (https://www.investopedia.com/terms/g/gbp.asp)

Group of 7 (G-7) – The Group of Seven (G-7) is a forum of the seven countries with the world's largest developed economies—**France, Germany, Italy, Japan,** the **United States,** the **United Kingdom,** and **Canada**—whose government leaders meet annually on international economic and monetary issues. The Presidency of the G-7 is held by each of the member countries in turn. The **European Union** is sometimes considered an eighth member of the G-7, since it holds all the rights and responsibilities of full members except to chair or host the meeting. (https://www.investopedia.com/terms/g/g7.asp)

H

Hedge funds – are alternative investments using pooled funds that employ different strategies to earn active return, or alpha, for their investors. Hedge funds may be aggressively managed or make use of derivatives and leverage in both domestic and international markets with the goal of generating high returns (either in an absolute sense or over a specified market benchmark). It is important to note that hedge funds are generally only accessible to accredited investors as they require less SEC regulations than other funds. One aspect that has set the hedge fund industry apart is the fact that hedge funds face less regulation than mutual funds and other investment vehicles. (https://www.investopedia.com/terms/h/hedgefund.asp)

I

Imbalance – (Imbalance of orders) is when too many orders of a particular type – either buy, sell or limit – for listed securities and not enough of the other, matching orders are received by an exchange. Imbalance of orders is also referred to as an "order imbalance." (https://www.investopedia.com/terms/i/imbalanceoforders.asp)

Index – is an indicator or measure of something, and in finance, it typically refers to a statistical measure of change in a securities market. In the case of financial markets, stock, and bond market indices consist of a hypothetical portfolio of securities representing a particular market or a segment of it. (You cannot invest directly in an index.) The S&P 500 and the US Aggregate Bond Index are common benchmarks for the American stock and bond markets, respectively. (https://www.investopedia.com/terms/i/index.asp)

Insider Trading – is the buying or selling of a publicly traded company's stock by someone who has non-public, material information about that stock. Insider trading can be illegal or legal depending on when the insider makes the trade. It is illegal when the material information is still non-public. (https://www.investopedia.com/terms/i/insidertrading.asp) **Link to real life events:** http://tbrnews.com/news/hermosa-beach-man-charged-with-insider-trading-while-working-as/article_b32bb2c2-0cc7-11ea-bd7e-57a14596d9de.html

Institutional Investor – is a nonbank person or organization that trades securities in large enough share quantities or dollar amounts that it qualifies for preferential treatment and lower commissions. An institutional investor is an organization that invests on behalf of its members. Institutional investors face fewer protective regulations because it is assumed they are more knowledgeable and better able to protect themselves. There are generally six types of institutional investors: **endowment funds, commercial banks, mutual funds, hedge funds, pension funds** and **insurance companies**. Institutional investors have the resources and specialized knowledge for extensively researching a variety of investment options not open to retail investors. Because institutions are the largest force behind supply and demand in securities markets, they perform the majority of trades on major exchanges and greatly influence the prices of securities. For this reason, retail investors often research institutional investors' regulatory filings with the Securities and Exchange Commission (SEC) to determine which securities the retail investors should buy personally. Retail investors typically do not invest in the same securities as institutional investors to avoid paying higher prices for the securities. (https://www.investopedia.com/terms/i/institutionalinvestor.asp)

Interbank Market – The interbank market is the global network utilized by financial institutions to trade currencies between themselves. While some interbank trading is done by banks on behalf of large customers, most interbank trading is proprietary, meaning that it takes place on behalf of the banks' own accounts. Banks use the interbank market to manage exchange rate and interest rate risk. **Basics of Interbank Market** → The interbank market for forex serves commercial turnover of currency investments as well as a large amount of speculative, short-term currency trading. Typical maturity term for transactions in the Interbank market is overnight or six months. According to data compiled in 2004 by the Bank for International Settlements, approximately 50% of all forex transactions are strictly interbank trades. A Brief History of the Interbank Market…

The interbank foreign exchange market developed after the collapse of the Bretton Woods agreement and following the decision by U.S. President Richard Nixon to take the country off the gold standard in 1971. Currency rates of most of the large industrialized nations were allowed to float freely at that point, with only occasional government intervention. There is no centralized location for the market, as trading takes place simultaneously around the world, and stops only for weekends and holidays. The advent of the floating rate system coincided with the emergence of low-cost computer systems that allowed increasingly rapid trading on a global basis. Voice brokers over telephone systems matched buyers and sellers in the early days of interbank forex trading but were gradually replaced by computerized systems that could scan large numbers of traders for the best prices. Trading systems from Reuters and Bloomberg allow banks to trade billions of dollars at once, with daily trading volume topping $6 trillion on the market's busiest days.

Largest Participants in the Interbank Market → In order to be considered an interbank market maker, a bank must be willing to make prices to other participants as well as asking for prices. The minimum size for an interbank deal is $5 million, but most transactions are much larger, and can top $1 billion in a single deal. Among the largest players are Citicorp and JP Morgan Chase in the United States, Deutsche Bank in Germany, and HSBC in Asia. There are several other participants in the interbank market, including trading firms and hedge funds. While they contribute to the setting of exchange rates through their purchase and sale operations, other participants do not have as much of an effect on currency exchange rates as large banks. (https://www.investopedia.com/terms/i/interbankmarket.asp)

Interest Rate - The amount a lender charges for the use of assets expressed as a percentage of the principal. The interest rate is typically noted on an annual basis known as the annual percentage rate (APR). The assets borrowed could include cash, consumer goods, or large assets such as a vehicle or building. The interest rate charged by banks is determined by a number of factors such as the state of the economy. A country's central bank sets the interest rate. When the central bank sets interest rates at a high level the cost of debt rises. When the cost of debt is high, thus discouraging people from borrowing and slows consumer demand. Also, interest rates tend to rise with inflation. (https://www.investopedia.com/terms/i/interestrate.asp)

Intermarket Analysis – A method of analyzing markets by examining the correlations between different asset classes. In other words, what happens in one market could, and probably does, affect other markets, so a study of the relationship(s) could prove to be beneficial to the trader. Intermarket analysis looks at more than one related asset class or financial market to determine the strength, or weakness, of the financial markets, or asset classes, being considered. Instead of looking at financial markets or asset classes on an individual basis, intermarket analysis looks at several strongly correlated markets, or asset classes, such as stocks, bonds, currencies, and commodities. This type of analysis expands on simply looking at each individual market or asset in isolation by also looking at other markets or assets that have a strong relationship to the market or asset being considered. For example, when studying the U.S. market, it is worthwhile to look at the U.S. bond market, commodity prices, and the U.S. Dollar. The changes in the related markets, such as commodity prices, may have an impact on the U.S. stock market and would need to be understood to obtain a greater understanding of the future direction of the U.S. stock market. Intermarket analysis should be considered fundamental analysis in that it relies more on relationships to provide a general sense of direction, but it is often classified as a branch of technical analysis. There are different approaches to intermarket analysis, including mechanical and rule based. (John J. Murphy is the "father of intermarket analysis" and we look to his guidance for explanation.) (https://www.investopedia.com/terms/i/intermarketanalysis.asp)

Book recommendations:

> *Intermarket Technical Analysis* by John J. Murphy
> *Currency Trading and Intermarket Analysis: How to profit from shifting currents in global markets* by Ashraf Laïdi (Wiley Trading Series)

K

Kiwi – The New Zealand dollar (NZD) is the currency of New Zealand. NZD is made up of 100 cents and is often represented by the symbol $ or NZ$ to set it apart from other currencies based in dollars. The money also sees use in the Cook Islands, Niue, Tokelau, and the Pitcairn Islands. The New Zealand Dollar is often commonly referred to as a kiwi because of the national bird found stamped on the one-dollar coin. (NZD/USD) Correlates strongly with AUD/USD and is used when identifying correlation divergences and used with intermarket technical analysis. XAU/NZD to compare the strength of NZD to Gold. (https://www.investopedia.com/terms/forex/n/nzd-new-zealand-dollar.asp)

L

Laggard – A laggard is a stock or security that is underperforming relative to its benchmark or peers. A laggard will have lower-than-average returns compared to the market. A laggard is the opposite of a leader. In most cases, a laggard refers to a stock. The term can also, however, describe a company or individual that has been underperforming. It is often used to describe good vs. bad, as in "leaders vs. laggards." Investors want to avoid laggards, because they achieve *less-than-desired rates of return*. In broader terms, the term laggard connotes resistance to progress and a persistent pattern of falling behind. As an example of a laggard, consider stock ABC that consistently posts annual returns of only 2 percent when other stocks in the industry post average returns of 5 percent. Stock ABC would be considered a laggard. (https://www.investopedia.com/terms/l/laggard.asp)

Liquid Market – A liquid market a market with many available buyers and sellers and comparatively low transaction costs. The details of what makes a market liquid may vary depending on the asset being exchanged. In a liquid market, it is easy to execute a trade quickly and at a desirable price because there are numerous buyers and sellers and the product being exchanged is standardized and in high demand. In a liquid market despite daily changes in

supply and demand the spread between what the buyer wants to pay and what sellers will offer remains relatively small. The opposite of a liquid market is called a "thin market" or an "illiquid market." Thin markets may have considerably large spreads between the highest available buyer and the lowest available seller. Liquid markets are usually found in financial assets such as forex, futures, bonds and stocks. Markets for high-priced tangible goods, such as luxury items, heavy industrial equipment or houses are considered illiquid markets. But even financial securities can also be thinly traded depending on a number of factors including the time of day, the immediate conditions of a given market, or the relative visibility of the asset. The market for the stock of a Fortune 500 company would be considered a liquid market, but the market for a family-owned restaurant would not. The largest and most liquid market in the world is the forex market, where foreign currencies are traded. It is estimated that the daily trading volume in the currency market is over $5 trillion, which is dominated by the U.S. dollar. The markets for the euro, yen, pound, franc, and Canadian dollar are also highly liquid.
(https://www.investopedia.com/terms/l/liquidmarket.asp)

Liquidity – describes the degree to which an asset or security can be quickly bought or sold in the market at a price reflecting its intrinsic value. In other words: the ease of converting it to cash. Cash is universally considered the most liquid asset, while tangible assets, such as real estate, fine art, and collectibles, are all relatively illiquid. Other financial assets, ranging from equities to partnership units, fall at various places on the liquidity spectrum.
(https://www.investopedia.com/terms/l/liquidity.asp)

M

Market Makers – The most common type of market maker is a brokerage house that provides purchase and sale solutions for investors in an effort to keep financial markets liquid. A market maker can also be an individual intermediary, but due to the size of securities needed to facilitate the volume of purchases and sales, the vast majority of market makers work on behalf of large institutions. "Making a market" signals a willingness to buy and sell the securities of a defined set of companies to broker-dealer firms that are member firms of that exchange. Each market maker displays buy and sell quotations for a guaranteed number of shares. Once an order is received from a buyer, the market maker immediately sells off his position of shares from his own inventory, to complete the order. In short, market making facilitates a smoother flow of financial markets by making it easier for investors and traders to buy and sell. Without market making, there may be insufficient transactions and less overall investment activities.
(https://www.investopedia.com/terms/m/marketmaker.asp)

Market Manipulation – Market manipulation refers to artificially inflating or deflating the price of a security or otherwise influencing the behavior of the market for personal gain. Manipulation is illegal in most cases, but it can be difficult for regulators and other authorities to detect, such as with omnibus accounts. Manipulation is also difficult for the manipulator as the size and number of participants in a market increase. It is much easier to manipulate the share price of smaller companies, such as penny stocks because analysts and other market participants do not watch them as closely as the medium and large-cap firms. Manipulation is variously called price manipulation, stock manipulation, and market manipulation. Currency manipulation is a slightly different class of market manipulation, as only central banks and national governments can engage in it, and they are legal authorities in and of themselves. Being the owner of a currency legitimizes many of the actions these governments take to suppress or inflate their currency's value compared to its peers. Even though currency manipulation is not illegal, a country that is manipulating its currency may be challenged by other nations or punished through sanctions passed by its trading partners. Moreover, international bodies like the World Trade Organization (WTO) have been encouraged to play a stronger role in addressing accusations of currency manipulation. Devaluation is the way to manipulate currency through the deliberate downward adjustment of the value of a country's money relative to another currency, group of currencies, or currency standard. The government issuing the currency decides to devalue a currency and, unlike depreciation, it is not the result of nongovernmental activities. One reason a country may devalue its currency is to combat a trade imbalance. Devaluation reduces the cost of a country's exports, rendering them more competitive in the global market, which in turn, increases the cost of imports, so domestic consumers are less likely to purchase them, further strengthening domestic businesses. Because exports increase and imports decrease, it favors a better balance of payments by shrinking trade deficits. That means a country that devalues its currency can reduce its deficit because of the strong demand for cheaper exports. (https://www.investopedia.com/terms/m/manipulation.asp)

Market order – is a request by an investor, usually made through a broker or brokerage service, to buy or sell a security at the best available price in the current market. It is widely considered the fastest and most reliable way to enter or exit a trade and provides the most likely method of getting in or out of a trade quickly. For many large-cap liquid stocks, market orders fill nearly instantaneously. (https://www.investopedia.com/terms/m/marketorder.asp)

Market Sentiment – refers to the overall attitude of investors toward a particular security or financial market. It is the feeling or tone of a market, or its crowd psychology, as revealed through the activity and price movement of the securities traded in that market. In broad terms, rising prices indicate bullish market sentiment, while falling prices indicate bearish market sentiment. (https://www.investopedia.com/terms/m/marketsentiment.asp)

Microeconomics – is the social science that studies the implications of human action, specifically about how those decisions affect the utilization and distribution of scarce resources. Microeconomics shows how and why different goods have different values, how individuals make more efficient or more productive decisions, and how individuals best coordinate and cooperate with one another. Generally speaking, microeconomics is considered a more complete, advanced, and settled science than macroeconomics. (https://www.investopedia.com/terms/m/microeconomics.asp)

N

Nasdaq 100 Index – is a basket of the 100 largest, most actively traded U.S companies listed on the Nasdaq stock exchange. The index includes companies from various industries except for the financial industry, like commercial and investment banks. These non-financial sectors include retail, biotechnology, industrial, technology, health care, and others. The Nasdaq 100 is traded through the Invesco QQQ Trust. This product is designed to track the performance of the 100 largest companies on the Nasdaq exchange. Each company in the trust must be a member of the Nasdaq 100 and be listed on the broader exchange for at least two years. Also, listed stocks need to have an average daily trading volume of 200,000 and publicly report earnings quarterly and annually. (https://www.investopedia.com/terms/n/nasdaq100.asp)

O

Open interest – is the total number of outstanding derivative contracts, such as options or futures that have not been settled for an asset. The total open interest does not count and total every buy and sell contract. Instead, open interest provides a more accurate picture of the options trading activity, and whether money flows into the futures and options market are increasing or decreasing. It's important to note that open interest equals the total number of contracts, not the total of each transaction by every buyer and seller. In other words, open interest is the total of all the buys or all of the sells, not both. The open interest number only changes when a new buyer and seller enter the market, creating a new contract, or when a buyer and seller meet—thereby closing both positions. For example, if one trader has ten contracts short (sale) and another has ten contracts long (purchase), and these traders then buy and sell ten contracts to each other, those contracts are now closed and will be deducted from open interest. (https://www.investopedia.com/terms/o/openinterest.asp)

Outperform – In financial news media Outperform is commonly used as a rating given by analysts who publicly research and recommend securities. If they change their rating on a particular security to "Outperform" from "Market Perform" or even "Underperform" then something has changed in their analysis that makes them believe the security will produce higher returns, for the foreseeable future, than the major market indexes. Another common usage of this term is as a description of how the returns of one investment compare to another. Between two investment choices, the one with better returns is said to outperform the other. This is most commonly applied to a comparison between one investment and the market in general. Investment professionals almost always compare investment returns with a benchmark index, such as the S&P 500 index, so the term is often used to in reference to whether a particular investment has outperformed the S&P 500. (https://www.investopedia.com/terms/o/outperform.asp)

P

Position trader refers to an individual who holds an investment for an extended period of time with the expectation that it will appreciate in value. The average time frames for holding positions can be measured in weeks to months. They are less concerned with short-term fluctuations and the news of the day unless it impacts the long-term view of their position. Position traders do not trade actively, with most placing less than 10 trades a year. (https://www.investopedia.com/terms/p/positiontrader.asp)

Price action – is the movement of a security's price plotted over time. Price action forms the basis for all technical analysis of a stock, commodity, or other asset chart. Many short-term traders rely exclusively on price action and the formations and trends extrapolated from it to make trading decisions. Technical analysis as a practice is a derivative of price action since it uses past prices in calculations that can then be used to inform trading decisions. (https://www.investopedia.com/terms/p/price-action.asp)

Q

Quantitative easing – (QE) is an unconventional monetary policy in which a central bank purchases government securities or other securities from the market in order to increase the money supply and encourage lending and investment. When short-term interest rates are at or approaching zero, normal open market operations, which target interest rates, are no longer effective, so instead a central bank can target specified amounts of assets to purchase. Quantitative easing increases the money supply by purchasing assets with newly created bank reserves in order to provide banks with more liquidity. (https://www.investopedia.com/terms/q/quantitative-easing.asp)

R

Relative strength – is a technique used in momentum investing. It consists of investing in securities that have performed well, relative to their market or benchmark. For example, a relative strength investor might select technology companies that have outperformed the Nasdaq Composite Index. **Not to be confused with the RSI (Relative Strength Index)** (https://www.investopedia.com/terms/r/relativestrength.asp)

Retail Investor – also known as an individual investor, is a non-professional investor who buys and sells securities, mutual funds, or exchange traded funds (ETFs) through traditional or online brokerage firms or other types of investment accounts. Retail investors purchase securities for their own personal accounts and often trade in dramatically smaller amounts as compared to institutional investors like pensions, endowments or mutual funds. By definition, the SEC considers retail investors unsophisticated investors, who are afforded certain protections and barred from making certain risky, complex investments. (https://www.investopedia.com/terms/r/retailinvestor.asp)

Risk – In broad terms, risk involves exposure to some type of danger and the possibility of loss or injury. In general, risks can apply to your physical health or job security. In finance and investing, risk often refers to the chance an outcome or investment's actual gains will differ from an expected outcome or return. Risk includes the possibility of losing some or all of an original investment. (https://www.investopedia.com/terms/r/risk.asp)

Risk-averse refers to investors who, when faced with two investments with a similar expected return, prefer the lower-risk option. Risk-averse can be contrasted with risk seeking. (https://www.investopedia.com/terms/r/riskaverse.asp)

Risk/reward ratio – marks the prospective reward an investor can earn, for every dollar he or she risks on an investment. Many investors use risk/reward ratios to compare the expected returns of an investment with the amount of risk they must undertake to earn these returns. Consider the following example: an investment with a risk-reward ratio of 1:7 suggests that an investor is willing to risk $1, for the prospect of earning $7. Alternatively, a risk/reward ratio of 1:3 signals that an investor should expect to invest $1, for the prospect of earning $3 on his investment. (https://www.investopedia.com/terms/r/riskrewardratio.asp)

S&P500 Index – is a market-capitalization-weighted index of the 500 largest U.S. publicly traded companies. The index is widely regarded as the best gauge of large-cap U.S. equities. $SPY (ETF) and ES1! (Futures) (https://www.investopedia.com/terms/s/sp500.asp)

Scalping – is a trading strategy geared towards profiting from minor price changes in a stock's price. Traders who implement this strategy place anywhere from 10 to a few hundred trades in a single day with the belief that small moves in stock price are easier to catch than large ones; traders who implement this strategy are known as scalpers. Many small profits can easily compound into large gains, if a strict exit strategy is used to prevent large losses. (https://www.investopedia.com/terms/s/scalping.asp)

Seasonality – is a characteristic of a time series in which the data experiences regular and predictable changes that recur every calendar year. Any predictable fluctuation or pattern that recurs or repeats over a one-year period is said to be seasonal. Seasonal effects are different from cyclical effects, as seasonal cycles are observed within one calendar year, while cyclical effects, such as boosted sales due to low unemployment rates, can span time periods shorter or longer than one calendar year. (Equityclock.com is a good place to find seasonal patterns for many assets.) (https://www.investopedia.com/terms/s/seasonality.asp)

Short – or a short position, is created when a trader sells a security first with the intention of repurchasing it or covering it later at a lower price. A trader may decide to short a security when she believes that the price of that security is likely to decrease in the near future. There are two types of short positions: naked and covered. A naked short is when a trader sells a security without having possession of it. However, that practice is illegal in the U.S. for equities. A covered short is when a trader borrows the shares from a stock loan department; in return, the trader pays a borrow-rate during the time the short position is in place. In the futures or foreign exchange markets, short positions can be created at any time. (https://www.investopedia.com/terms/s/short.asp)

Short squeeze – is a situation in which a heavily shorted stock or commodity moves sharply higher, forcing short sellers to close out their short positions and adding to the upward pressure on the stock. Short sellers are being squeezed out of their short positions, usually at a loss. Short squeezes are generally triggered by a positive development that suggests the stock may be embarking on a turnaround. Although the turnaround in the stock's fortunes may only prove to be temporary, few short sellers can afford to risk runaway losses on their short positions and may prefer to close the position even if it means taking a substantial loss. (https://www.investopedia.com/terms/s/shortsqueeze.asp)

Slippage – refers to the difference between the expected price of a trade and the price at which the trade is executed. Slippage can occur at any time but is most prevalent during periods of higher volatility when market orders are used. It can also occur when a large order is executed but there isn't enough volume at the chosen price to maintain the current bid/ask spread. (https://www.investopedia.com/terms/s/slippage.asp)

Smart money – is the capital that is being controlled by **institutional investors, market mavens, central banks, funds, and other financial professionals**. Smart money was originally a gambling term that referred to the wagers made by gamblers with a track record of success. Usually, these gamblers had deep knowledge of the sport they were betting on or insider knowledge that the public was unable to tap into. The investing world is similar. The populace perceives that the smart money is invested by those with a fuller understanding of the market or with information that a regular investor cannot access. As such, the smart money is considered to have a much better chance of success when the trading patterns of institutional investors diverge from retail investors. **Smart money is cash invested or wagered by those considered experienced, well informed, "in-the-know," or all three.** There is little empirical evidence to support the notion that smart-money investments perform better than non-smart-money investments; however, such influxes of cash influence many speculation methods. (https://www.investopedia.com/terms/s/smart-money.asp)

Spread – can have several meanings in finance. Basically, however, they all refer to the difference between two prices, rates or yields. In one of the most common definitions, the spread is the gap between the bid and the ask prices of a security or asset, like a stock, bond or commodity. This is known as a bid-ask spread. (https://www.investopedia.com/terms/s/spread.asp)

Stop-loss order – is an order placed with a broker to buy or sell a security when it reaches a certain price. Stop-loss orders are designed to limit an investor's loss on a position in a security and are different from stop-limit orders. When a stock falls below the stop price the order becomes a market order and it executes at the next available price. For example, a trader may buy a stock and places a stop-loss order 10% below the purchase price. Should the stock drop, the stop-loss order would be activated, and the stock would be sold as a market order. (https://www.investopedia.com/terms/s/stop-lossorder.asp)

Swap – is a derivative contract through which two parties exchange the cash flows or liabilities from two different financial instruments. Most swaps involve cash flows based on a notional principal amount such as a loan or bond, although the instrument can be almost anything. Usually, the principal does not change hands. Each cash flow comprises one leg of the swap. One cash flow is generally fixed, while the other is variable and based on a benchmark interest rate, floating currency exchange rate or index price. The most common kind of swap is an interest rate swap. Swaps do not trade on exchanges, and retail investors do not generally engage in swaps. Rather, swaps are over-the-counter contracts primarily between businesses or financial institutions that are customized to the needs of both parties. (https://www.investopedia.com/terms/s/swap.asp)

Swing trading – is a style of trading that attempts to capture gains in a stock (or any financial instrument) over a period of a few days to several weeks. Swing traders primarily use technical analysis to look for trading opportunities. These traders may utilize fundamental analysis in addition to analyzing price trends and patterns. (https://www.investopedia.com/terms/s/swingtrading.asp)

T

Take-profit order (T/P) – is a type of limit order that specifies the exact price at which to close out an open position for a profit. (https://www.investopedia.com/terms/t/take-profitorder.asp)

Technical analysis – is a trading discipline employed to evaluate investments and identify trading opportunities by analyzing statistical trends gathered from trading activity, such as price movement and volume. Unlike fundamental analysts, who attempt to evaluate a security's intrinsic value, technical analysts focus on patterns of price movements, trading signals and various other analytical charting tools to evaluate a security's strength or weakness. (https://www.investopedia.com/terms/t/technicalanalysis.asp)

Top-down analysis – looks at the "big picture" first for an investment idea or selection of stocks. After stocks have been identified as ideally placed to benefit from global trend, then the analyst will look into the actual details and balance sheets of this subset to make a final investment decision. (https://www.investopedia.com/terms/t/topdownanalysis.asp)

U

Underperform – If an investment is underperforming, it is not keeping pace with other securities. In a rising market, for example, a stock is underperforming if it is not experiencing gains equal to or greater to the advance in the S&P 500 Index. In a down market, a stock that is a falling faster than the broader market is an underperformer. "Underperform" is also an analyst recommendation assigned to a stock when shares are expected to do slightly worse than the market return. The designation is also known as market "moderate sell" or "weak hold." (https://www.investopedia.com/terms/u/underperform.asp)

V

VIX – Created by the Chicago Board Options Exchange (CBOE), the Volatility Index, or VIX, is a real-time market index that represents the market's expectation of 30-day forward-looking volatility. Derived from the price inputs of the S&P 500 index options, it provides a measure of market risk and investors' sentiments. It is also known by other names like "Fear Gauge" or "Fear Index." Investors, research analysts and portfolio managers look to VIX values as a way to measure market risk, fear and stress before they take investment decisions. (https://www.investopedia.com/terms/v/vix.asp)

Volatility – is a statistical measure of the dispersion of returns for a given security or market index. In most cases, the higher the volatility, the riskier the security. Volatility is often measured as either the standard deviation or variance between returns from that same security or market index. In the securities markets, volatility is often associated with big swings in either direction. For example, when the stock market rises and falls more than one percent over a sustained period of time, it is called a "volatile" market. An asset's volatility is a key factor when pricing options contracts. (https://www.investopedia.com/terms/v/volatility.asp)

Volume – is the number of shares or contracts traded in a security or an entire market during a given period of time. For every buyer, there is a seller, and each transaction contributes to the count of total volume. That is, when buyers and sellers agree to make a transaction at a certain price, it is considered one transaction. If only five transactions occur in a day, the volume for the day is five. (https://www.investopedia.com/terms/v/volume.asp)

W

Wall Street – is a street located in the lower Manhattan section of New York City and is the home of the New York Stock Exchange or NYSE. Wall Street has also been the historic headquarters of some of the largest U.S. brokerages and investment banks. (https://www.investopedia.com/terms/w/wallstreet.asp)

Whipsaw – describes the movement of a security when, at a particular time, the security's price is moving in one direction but then quickly pivots to move in the opposite direction. There are two types of whipsaw patterns. The first involves an upward movement in a share price, which is then followed by a drastic downward move causing the share's price to fall relative to its original position. The second type occurs when a share price drops in value for a short time and then suddenly surges upward to a positive gain relative to the stock's original position. (https://www.investopedia.com/terms/w/whipsaw.asp)

All References

Angell, George. Winning in the Commodities Market: A Moneymaking Guide to Commodity

Futures Trading. Doubleday & Co, 1979.

Banton, Caroline. "Smart Money Is Invested by Those in the Know." Investopedia, Investopedia,

29 Jan. 2020, www.investopedia.com/terms/s/smart-money.asp.

Barchart.com

Beta, Toba. Master of Stupidity. 2011.

Chen, James. "Institutional Investor." Investopedia, Investopedia, 29 Jan. 2020,

www.investopedia.com/terms/i/institutionalinvestor.asp.

Coghlan, Giles. "How the US Dollar Index Can Help Your Trading." ForexLive,

www.forexlive.com/Education/!/how-the-us-dollar-index-can-help-your-trading-20190126.

Commodity Futures Trading Commission. https://www.cftc.gov/

Douglas, M. (1990). *The disciplined trader: Developing winning attitudes*. New York, NY: New York Institute of finance.

Douglas, M. (2000). *Trading in the Zone: Master the Market with Confidence, Discipline, and a Winning Attitude*. New York, NY: New York Institute of Finance.

Douglas, M., & Webb, P. T. (2020). *The Complete Trader: The Definitive Guide to Mastering the Psychology of Market Behavior*. USA: Global Publishing House. Retrieved August 20, 2020, from https://www.amazon.com/Complete-Trader-Definitive-Mastering-Psychology-ebook/dp/B088CRBGZ4

Ganti, A. (2020, August 01). How Open Interest is Determined.

https://www.investopedia.com/terms/o/openinterest.asp

Hill, N., 1999. Success Through A Positive Mental Attitude. Sydney: HarperBusiness.

Hill, N., 1999. *Success Through A Positive Mental Attitude*. Sydney: HarperBusiness.

Koyenikan, Idowu. *Wealth for All: Living a Life of Success at the Edge of Your Ability*. Grandeur Touch, LLC, 2016.

Reuters. "U.S. Charges Another Ex-JPMorgan Executive with Alleged Market Manipulation." 16 Nov. 2019, www.reuters.com/article/us-usa-metals-charges/u-s-charges-another-ex-jpmorgan-executive-with-alleged-market-manipulation-idUSKBN1XP2FQ.

Russell, John. "Prevent Losses in Your Forex Trading." *The Balance*, The Balance, 25 June 2019, www.thebalance.com/why-do-forex-traders-lose-money-1344936.

Sanderson, Henry. "Three JPMorgan Metals Traders Charged with Market Manipulation." *Subscribe to Read | Financial Times*, Financial Times, 16 Sept. 2019, www.ft.com/content/2d7be5a6-d87a-11e9-8f9b-77216ebe1f17.

Segal, Troy. "Forex Folk: Who Trades Currency and Why." *Investopedia*, 29 Jan. 2020, www.investopedia.com/articles/forex/11/who-trades-forex-and-why.asp.

Williams, L. R. (1979). *How I made one million dollars last year trading commodities*. Brightwaters, NY: Windsor Books.

Williams, L. R. (1986). *The secret of selecting stocks for immediate and substantial gains*. Brightwaters, NY: Windsor Books.

Yotov, Ilian. *The Quarters Theory: The Revolutionary New Foreign Currencies Trading Method*. Wiley, 2010.

Useful Web Sources

www.barchart.com

www.cftc.gov

www.cmegroup.com

www.equityclock.com

www.forexfactory.com

www.investopedia.com

www.marketwatch.com

www.mrci.com

www.myfxbook.com

www.tradingview.com

Thanks for reading my first book!

Let me know what you think by sending a message to @jonfibonacci on Instagram!

You can also connect with me through other social media:

https://www.youtube.com/jonfibonacci

https://www.tradingview.com/u/JonFibonacci/

Manufactured by Amazon.ca
Bolton, ON

25979751R00093